LEARNING TO COPE

HUMAN HORIZONS SERIES

LEARNING
TO COPE

Edward Whelan & Barbara Speake

A CONDOR BOOK
SOUVENIR PRESS (E&A) LTD

List of figures and tables

Graphic art and cover photograph by Terry Speake.

Illustrations by Edward Whelan

Contents

Preface

This book provides an opportunity for us to draw together the experiences and ideas which we have gained during several years of research into the needs of mentally handicapped adolescents and adults.

As a result of our work, we are very optimistic about what can be achieved when careful thought is given to the learning situation. We have been impressed by the dedication and ingenuity of many parents and by the enthusiasm and commitment of staff. Many of the ideas which we present in the book have arisen from our numerous contacts with them as well as from our reading and research. We dedicate this book to them and hope that it will provide further illustration of the tremendous scope which now exists for closer partnership.

Handicapped adolescents are usually restricted in those experiences which are essential to the formation of a mature responsible adult. In the first chapter we explore the importance of this stage of development and consider the views of handicapped individuals themselves, as well as those of professionals and parents.

In Chapter 2 we take a closer look at the nature of learning difficulty and attempt to make this vague term more easily understood. In describing the basic mechanism, we stress the similarities of the way in which we all learn. The areas which research has shown to produce difficulties for mentally handicapped people are then briefly reviewed and may be seen in a new perspective. In Chapter 3 we provide a checklist to enable you as parents to assess for yourselves the degree to which your handicapped youngster is able to cope with the demands of everyday life. This checklist offers both a means of recording the level of ability, and also the extent to which

A*

particular abilities are actually put to use. The completed checklist forms a basis for deciding which goals may be set for training the individual and for setting priorities which take account of his or her strengths and interests. The principles involved in choosing a goal, bearing in mind the need to maintain a balance of priorities among the competing needs of the individual, are fully described in Chapter 4.

Before embarking on a description of how to teach, we want you to prepare your resources – to discover what opportunities exist both in the home and in your neighbourhood. How to set about this, including the creation of new opportunities where necessary, is described in Chapter 5.

In Chapter 6 we provide a detailed, step by step, account of how to apply the most powerful techniques of teaching which research has shown to be successful. We show you how to be more precise in defining your objectives, breaking down a task into stages; various ways of demonstrating the activity; and the effective use of rewards. We show you how to plan your work, setting target dates for the achievement of various stages of the task. In this section we describe special techniques to apply to the 'behaviour problems' which parents often describe as their chief concern.

The need to record progress, and the methods by which this may be accomplished, are fully described in Chapter 7. Having selected your targets, and decided upon your teaching plan, we invite you to devise teaching schemes incorporating the exercises presented in Chapters 8, 9 and 10. These deal with the three main aspects of 'coping': self-help, social academic, and interpersonal skills.

In Chapter 11 we stop and review progress. How successful have the teaching plans been? What new objectives or strategies are needed? Can resources be used more effectively? In describing how to carry out such a review we discuss the importance of checking that your son or daughter can apply new knowledge and skills in different settings. Some exercises are suggested which aim to test this.

In the last chapter, we take a look at the overall context in which the ideas and activities described in this book should be seen. We left this overview until the end because we feel that your own role within it might have become clearer by this stage. We show you how to relate your own efforts to those of professionals, and build up a sound network of support and help, ensuring that your son or daughter continues to make the fullest use of his or her abilities.

This book is written at a time when changes are occurring more rapidly than at any other time in the history of our services. We describe the newly emerging, more progressive, philosophy of provision for mentally handicapped adolescents and adults. Many major reports have been, or are about to be published. We hope that this book will contribute in some way towards even greater optimism about what may be achieved when love and dedication are guided by the application of sound principles derived both from research and examples of good practice.

1 The need for a book about 'coping'

This is a book about coping. Our focus is on the needs of mentally handicapped adolescents and adults, and our aim is to provide material that will be useful to parents, and also to others who are responsible for helping handicapped people to learn to cope successfully in the community. We draw on those areas which research and practice have shown to be most important to the encouragement of self-reliance and social independence.

LEARNING TO COPE arises directly from our own experience of working closely with parents and professionals over a period of several years. The book provides an opportunity for us to respond to a need we have come to recognise, and to bring together the experience and ideas which we have gained. We wish to share our optimism about what can be achieved when careful thought is given to the learning situation.

Many books already exist concerned with prevailing theories of handicap, the content of curriculum, or educational technology. We acknowledge our debt to these, and don't wish to duplicate them – we wish to supplement them, using language the layman can understand. We know that our readers would want to be guided by sound principles, but that technical jargon makes reading a chore rather than a pleasure. We are writing the book for parents in order to affirm our belief in the primary role which they play as educators of their children. We hope that the material will provide a basis for better collaboration between parents and professionals, many of whom should also find it useful.

We are deeply aware of the concern which many parents

have expressed about the period of adolescence and the transition to adulthood. We agree that this period presents special problems for the young person, and for the parent, and that it has been much neglected in the past. At the present time, however, this age group is beginning to receive more attention from experts, from those responsible for planning services, and from research workers. There is evidence, for example, that adolescence is a time of continued *intellectual* development, in addition to the rapid physical development which may be more obvious. Let us begin, then, by regarding adolescence as a time of great opportunity. We can assure you that your efforts at this stage will be well rewarded.

Many parents continue to talk of their 'child' for many years beyond the age when this term should have been discarded. This is understandable; but it does in fact inhibit the young person from assuming a new, adult role. It is widely accepted by experts that all of us identify with the role which our parents expect us to play – some research at the John Hopkins University, for example, suggests that as early as the age of two years a child has identified its sex as a result of the way in which the parents behave towards it. It is no less true of our adolescents that their efforts to be accepted as adults will be best rewarded by their acceptance by other adults, just as non-handicapped youngsters entering industry very quickly learn to imitate the behaviour of their older workmates. If you want your son or daughter to behave like an adult, then you simply must treat him or her as one.

Every human being is a unique individual, and every family is unique in its membership, and in the relationships among its members. This is equally true of handicapped individuals, and of their families. One of the difficulties, therefore, in writing a book such as the present one is that the authors cannot meet you or your handicapped son or daughter. We have to make certain assumptions, and we have to rely on you to apply or adapt the ideas we are going to present. Our

main assumption concerns your love, and your commitment
to help.

We hope to provide you with a unique opportunity to discover just what your son or daughter's current abilities or
strengths are. We show you how to set about selecting teaching objectives which you can work on in the home. We
are not afraid that you will become cold and clinical
in applying the principles of observation and teaching described – we have faith in your common sense. Our goal is
simply to help you to develop a more structured approach to
the task.

We show you how to design a programme and to carry
this out, and in particular how to make the most effective
use of everyday events in the home, and of opportunities in
your neighbourhood. We show you how to keep records, and
how to use them to check that you are making progress. By
numerous examples, we provide models for you to follow
when working on goals of your own choice. Throughout
the book, we require that you take your son's or daughter's
own feelings and wishes into account. It is vital that he
or she should be closely involved with each stage of the
process.

As your son or daughter learns to cope more and more, we
believe that this will reward your efforts. Life should become
easier in the home, and your relationship with him or her
should improve as greater maturity is attained and the adult
person emerges more clearly.

You should begin by accepting that your son and daughter is a person first, and a handicapped person second. We
no longer believe that being mentally handicapped dooms an
individual to a useless, unproductive, or unhappy life. In all
essential respects such a person is the same as any of us, and
we all prefer to think positively about ourselves. Throughout
this book we stress the individual's strengths and achievements, building upon these. This is known as the 'habilitation'
philosophy, it may be regarded as a continuation of the

educational philosophy underlying the teaching which your child received at school. It always attempts to see a problem in positive terms. Thus, instead of speaking of what a person cannot do, for instance, we say that he has *not yet learned* to do this.

What we hope to do in this book is to put the findings of research to practical use. We have been concerned for a long time about the gap which has developed between research and practice. It is now no longer believed, for example, that early learning is so critical – it is known that a good deal does and should continue to be learned well into adulthood. Many of the techniques which research has developed have been particularly applied to children – we intend to adapt them and make them suitable for use with young adults.

The greatest advance in our understanding of mental handicap came about when we began to regard such individuals as having a 'learning difficulty'. We stopped calling them 'patients', treating them as though they were ill, and accepted that their needs were educational. Over twenty years ago, pioneer work in this country showed just what could be achieved when sound principles of teaching are applied. It is now universally accepted that almost all human behaviour is learned. Unacceptable behaviour should not be thought of as an inevitable result of being handicapped.

It is known that mentally handicapped individuals usually have difficulty in learning 'incidentally' – that is, simply from experience. Yet we are sure that you could give many examples of things that your son or daughter *is* able to learn. Many will be able to relate in detail the events of last year's holiday, of a favourite TV programme, sing the words of a song, or hum a popular tune. Thus the problem is not usually *whether* a person can learn, but *what* they learn, and especially to what *use* they put this learning. Much of the knowledge and skill they must learn if they are to cope as independently as possible will not be acquired without instruction. It needs to be presented to them carefully and systematically. Once they have learned something, however, research has shown that they can remember it just as well as you or I, if not better.

As a result of our experience with seven 'workshops' for parents of mentally handicapped children and adults, we are convinced that much can be achieved when parents simply exchange views and ideas with other parents. We have been greatly impressed by the sound common sense and the ingenuity which many parents have demonstrated in applying the learning principles which we are to describe in this book. A common difficulty, however, is the problem of where to begin. Many parents ask 'Where shall I start, what is it most important for me to do?' Some express concern about the time scale, and about what they might expect to achieve: 'I don't mind how long it takes if it will be worth it in the long run.'

This is why we hope that this book will help you to focus your efforts and be sure of your direction. In order to experience success, you will be shown how to start with small steps, breaking behaviour down into its component parts and setting goals which can be achieved within a short time, usually within a week. Ultimately, the amount achieved will be proportional to the contribution you are able to make, and in the long term will depend upon the co-operative network of support and the partnerships which you establish, especially with professionals, within your neighbourhood.

For the young person concerned, it is important that learning should be fun. Just as children learn a great deal through play, so do adults learn a great deal during their recreation, engaging in games and projects which present them with a challenge. Research has clearly shown us the powerful effects of presenting demands. Recent research has shown that the experience of achievement, of learning something previously thought to be too difficult, provides the strongest possible reward for the behaviour concerned. Satisfaction from mastery and performance of the task itself is far stronger than any external rewards, in the form of praise, sweets, tokens, and so on. When given a choice between performing a complex assembly job without pay, and doing a simple repetitive task with pay, most mentally handicapped adults quickly chose the former. Indeed, a good deal is now being learned about the views and aspirations of mentally handicapped people: simply because we have begun asking them!

The Views of Mentally Handicapped Individuals

A recent American study on a project for discharging mentally handicapped adults from hospital into the community found that the individuals involved had many views to express. Those responsible for the project eventually concluded that the mentally handicapped individuals themselves should have acted as *consultants* to the project! Many of the problems which developed later could have been avoided if those concerned had been asked for their ideas and preferences.

Until quite recently it has been assumed that mentally handicapped individuals either do not hold views, or possess aspirations, or else they would be unable to express them anyhow. Only within the last decade have we heard of conferences convened for the exchange of views *between* mentally handicapped people. But there have been many conferences for professionals, and others, which have discussed their problems in their absence.

It is true that many mentally handicapped people have difficulty in communicating, in addition to being shy, when questioned by a stranger. But these problems are much less likely to arise in communication with parents or members of the family. You may not even realise the extent to which your long relationship has helped you to understand each other. Whilst you should not encourage poor speech habits by making too many allowances for them, clearly you are in a good position to encourage your son or daughter to express feelings and ideas.

It seems that the incidence of speech difficulties is indeed larger than once thought: a recent assessment by a speech therapist in two typical Adult Training Centres showed that over half the trainees showed some indication of faulty articulation. But even where articulation is a serious problem, we should persevere. New methods of communication have recently been tried which do not require spoken replies. Asked how he or she feels about something, the individual can for instance be taught how to respond by moving a simple pointer on a scale.

We have recently used a simple 'choice-box' as a means of discovering how some two hundred young people feel about themselves. They were nearly all mildly or moderately mentally handicapped, and the questions were concerned with how they saw themselves as workers. We will describe this technique in Chapter 10. For now, we should simply report that we ourselves were extremely impressed with how reliable their responses were. They were closely in agreement with staff ratings of their work performance.

In your own home, think about what opportunities exist for discovering the views of your mentally handicapped son or daughter. Look back to your own adolescence, and perhaps you will recall the periods of uncertainty and frustration which accompanied your attempts to express an independent personality. You may recall your teens as a time of idealism and impatience, of challenging authority and value systems. They were certainly a time of increasing responsibility, with opportunities for travel from home, a widening circle of friends and acquaintances, and access to new and often overwhelming working and social environments. How does your son or daughter feel about leaving school, what are his or her hopes for the future?

We interviewed a large number of young people attending Adult Training Centres about these and similar questions. In order to make conversation easier, we began by showing them black and white photographs of young people of a similar age to themselves working on simple tasks. They were asked to discuss the person in the picture, the work being carried out, whether he had any friends or not, and so on. Each individual was also asked whether he would like to be the person in the picture or not. The replies were tape recorded and were later analysed. In this way it was possible to discover the main preoccupations, the anxieties and hopes, of those taking part. Here is one response:

> It looks as though she (the woman in the photograph) is going to cry, because she's looking at the time on her watch. She is upset because she does not like the job, therefore she looks at her watch. She is bored stiff.

The greatest single preoccupation was with the family and the home. This was followed by a large number of varied interests, differing among individuals. Other concerns were about health, friendship, danger, and fear of failure. When asked their reason for being at the Centre, a large number of the young ladies interviewed replied: 'just until I get married.' However, the proportion leaving the Centre for this reason is very small indeed.

We know that one of the most difficult problems for parents is the absence of any yardstick for comparing development. When the child was younger, you were probably given very little idea of what to expect in the way of development, or of the time-scale within which to expect it, and, like many other parents, you may have been simply grateful for any help that was offered. In the light of this, few of you may feel in a position to question the stage that your son or daughter has reached, or to challenge the effectiveness of the education or training which has been provided. It is for this reason that we feel it might be useful for you to have an opportunity to learn something of the general level of attainment of other mentally handicapped adults attending Adult Training Centres. In the next section we will present some of the findings of the recent National Survey of Adult Training Centres, which the authors carried out, supported by a grant from the Department of Health and Social Security.

Survey Findings Concerning Level of Attainment

The following table, based on Table 56 of the National Survey Report, is a summary of the attainments of over 24,000 trainees. The figures are based on assessments carried out by the Centre staff, and provide a broad indication of the percentage of trainees who are considered to be capable, or not yet capable, of the abilities listed.

Table 1: SUMMARY OF EDUCATIONAL AND SOCIAL ATTAINMENT

Abilities	Percentage of trainees who have this ability	Percentage who do not yet have this ability	Not known at present
Talk in sentences	68.9%	13.9%	17.2%
Show normal courtesies	62.0	12.1	26.0
Recognise colours	59.0	20.0	21.0
Honesty	53.0	10.6	36.5
Personal hygiene	52.0	22.0	26.0
Signature	40.6	37.0	22.5
Counting and measuring	37.5	41.0	21.6
Telling the time	34.1	42.8	23.2

Abilities	Percentage of trainees who have this ability	Percentage who do not yet have this ability	Not known at present
*Writing	28.7	48.4	22.9
*Use of money, including budgeting	28.3	53.5	18.2
*Health hazards (knowledge of)	28.1	38.0	33.9
*Public transport	27.5	50.4	22.2
*Reading	25.8	53.0	21.2
*Prepare basic meal (including shopping	23.5	50.6	25.9
*Use of telephone (including emergency)	23.0	54.6	22.5
*General post office procedures	20.6	53.3	26.2
*Sexual responsibility	18.8	27.6	53.6
*Can take medicine by self, when required	18.1	46.4	35.6
*Use of medical, dental, social services	17.0	49.0	34.1
*Could live on own	6.0	63.2	30.7

Taken from Table 56, *Adult Training Centres in England and Wales Report of the First National Survey* (1977). Data is based on 24,252 trainees.

It should be noted from the table that fewer than a third of the trainees were considered at that time to possess many of the abilities which are particularly important for independent functioning in the community. We have indicated these twelve items by an asterisk. It can also be seen that these same items also account for the greatest percentage of 'not known', showing that a good deal more assessment is needed in these vital areas. You may wish to return to this table after reading the next chapter, in which we list many of the areas which research has identified as particularly important for coping alone in the community.

It can be seen from the table that only 6 per cent of trainees were thought by the staff to be capable of living on their own. This table, in association with the research findings reported in the next chapter, has greatly influenced the assessment scale which we have designed for you to apply. You will find this in Chapter 3.

There are many other findings from the National Survey which are of relevance to parents. We found, for example, that over 74 per cent of trainees are under the age of 35 years, and that 80 per cent of them live at home with their family. Although 94 per cent of Adult Training Centres say that they inform parents of their aims, fewer than 2 per cent say that they offer a counselling or advice service for parents. Despite this, as will be seen in Chapter 12, rapid developments are now taking place in these Centres.

The Survey has shown that staff appreciate the need for developing their social training programmes. This was what they most frequently set down as the use to which they would put a new member of staff. Indeed, training in social competence tops the list of those areas where they feel that further emphasis is necessary for those trainees 'who might become capable of employment'. There is also an urgent need for staff and parents to work more closely together, for although over 83 per cent of Centres say that the parents of their trainees belong to an organised group, it emerged that parental contact with the Centre was usually only a social one.

The importance of involving the family closely in training is further stressed in our finding that 'lack of support by the family' was the fourth most frequent reason given for individuals returning to the Centre from open employment. We feel that parents can do much to prepare their son or daughter for attendance at a Centre by the example and supervision which they provide in the home. This is particularly true in the case of individuals who show behaviour problems, and a section is devoted to this in Chapter 6. We found that the reason given most frequently by Centre staff for not wishing to accept an applicant in the ATC was the presence of a 'behaviour problem'.

In this section, together with the next chapter, you should begin to obtain an impression of the areas which professionals consider to be training priorities when developing 'coping' skills. We know that you will have your own ideas concerning such priorities, but, as pointed out earlier, you may find the views of other parents helpful. You may often have asked yourself: 'Am I being reasonable, do I still treat him like a child? Should I be taking more risks? If we don't help him to stand more on his own feet, what will happen when we're gone?'

These are important questions, made more difficult by the absence of a yardstick against which to compare your own relationship with your son or daughter. Faced with rapid development during adolescence, and possibly under pressure from those around you urging a less protective relationship, you may find this whole period quite stressful.

Views of Other Parents
The authors have recently carried out, for the Manpower Services Commission, a survey and evaluation of Young Persons' Work Preparation Courses.*

These courses, located in Employment Rehabilitation Centres, last three months. They are intended for youngsters who are educationally disadvantaged, mostly falling within the range of mild, or moderate, mental handicap. The aims of the Courses were described as:

*The full report of this study, entitled 'Young Persons' Work Preparation Courses – a Systematic Evaluation' may be obtained free of charge by writing to: The Chief Psychologist, Employment Service Division, 7 St Martin's Place, London.

Primarily to assist school leavers who because they are physically or mentally handicapped are unlikely to be settled into permanent employment without some form of preparation for the conditions they will meet when entering it.

As part of our evaluation of the effectiveness of these courses, parents of the youngsters concerned were asked to indicate how often certain behaviours were shown in the home. They were also given an opportunity to say how often they would like the behaviour to occur. In other words they were expected to say, in the light of their knowledge of their own son or daughter, what they thought would be reasonable to expect. The items which we selected were carefully chosen for their relevance both to the world of work and to the whole area of independent functioning.

The parents were asked to respond simply by placing a number in the box provided beside each item. The number, from 1-8, referred to a simple scale of frequency, from 'never' to 'more than once a day'. This can best be illustrated by presenting an example of a response to one of the items in the space below.

Statement	Answer	This is how often it happens (fill in number)	This is how often I would like it to happen (fill in number)
Helps with routine tasks at home, like cleaning up his room etc.	1. Never 2. Few times a year 3. Once a month 4. Few times a month 5. Once a week 6. Few times a week 7. Once a day 8. More than once a day	1.	5.

In this example, we can see that the parent has filled in number 1 in the first box and number 5 in the second box. This means that at the present time the youngster never helps with routine tasks at home, though the parent thinks it would be reasonable to expect this about once a week. There were sixteen items altogether, and we are going to show you how often, on average, parents said that their youngster actually showed the behaviour concerned, and in each case how often they thought they would like it to happen. You can see the results in Figure 1.

Bearing in mind that the youngsters concerned were all aged about sixteen years, and were mostly mildly handicapped, the bar-graph should give you some idea of the level of agreement among parents of educationally disadvantaged youngsters about how often certain behaviour might reasonably be expected. We see that these parents would prefer eight of the behaviours to be shown more frequently. In particular, they would like the youngsters to go out alone, to talk over their troubles, and to tackle new situations by themselves, much more often.

To give you some idea of what parents felt the effect of the course had been, we quote from some of their comments:

Has come out of his shell;
more interested in things;
now more keen to learn;
more independent behaviour, has applied for a job by himself;
noticed a marked improvement in the attitude of my son, since commencing on the course has been happy and much more independent;
made progress towards adulthood since starting the course, he has gained in confidence and now finds it easier to make decisions;
given son the opportunity to experience the difference between work and school work, now appreciates the length of the working day;
more independent financially, realises his limitations;
shoulders more responsibility.

Like these parents, you may have clear aspirations for

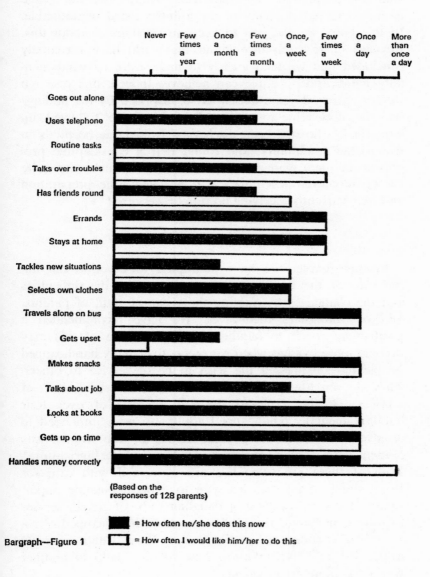

(Based on the
responses of 128 parents)

■ = How often he/she does this now

□ = How often I would like him/her to do this

Bargraph—Figure 1

your son or daughter. You may feel, however, that the degree of handicap makes many of the abilities listed unattainable. In this book we ask you to keep an open mind about this. Reviews of research throughout the world have repeatedly concluded that we tend greatly to under-estimate what mentally handicapped people can achieve. Indeed, one research worker, over 50 years ago, was so surprised by his findings that he was reluctant to publish them. He followed up individuals who had been discharged from large hospitals to live in the community, and found that a considerable proportion of them managed to remain in the community quite successfully even when they had received little preparation and were currently receiving no support services!

In this chapter we have attempted to describe the importance of the adolescent stage, illustrating the difficulties and the challenges by quoting the views of staff, of parents, and of youngsters themselves. We have recommended a positive approach to handicap, and the force of this may become more evident when we report that many handicapped people have expressed the wish to be of service to others. They do not always want to be on the 'receiving end' of services. Having explored the job interests of over four hundred mentally handicapped adults, we were impressed to discover that the most popular choice by the women was 'patient care', and by the men was 'horticulture/agriculture'. Both of these job categories are concerned with care for living things. Later, we ask you to explore possible opportunities for your own son or daughter to be of greater service to others, including those who are more handicapped. As a youngster attending a Spastics Society Work Centre recently said: 'I would like to know how to offer help to another worker, without giving offence.'

We expect that many of you, at this stage, will be anxious

to begin work. Some of you may wish to jump straight to Chapter 3 where we describe how to assess your son's or daughter's current abilities and training needs. We would recommend, however, that you read the next chapter first, which aims to give you a better understanding of what it means to be a 'slow learner'.

2 What does being a 'slow learner' mean?

The primary characteristic of mentally handicapped individuals is that they do not learn as readily as do others of the same age. We speak of such persons as having 'learning difficulties', or being 'slow learners.' In the international classification of handicap, the term 'retarded' is used. Although such terms are a great improvement on the dreadful labels which were used in former years, they do not adequately describe the problem. It is not so much the *rate* of learning that is important, but what is learned, and how this learning takes place. In this Chapter, we examine the learning process itself in order to show the many different ways in which 'learning difficulty' may be experienced.

We feel that you will find it worthwhile to grasp a basic understanding of the learning process at this stage in the book. The later sections concerned with assessment and particularly the techniques of teaching should subsequently make more sense. We have already said that every person is a unique individual. We have just stated that learning difficulty can take a number of forms. It follows from this that you need to know more than simply 'your son/daughter has a learning difficulty'. If you are to select the most effective teaching strategy, then you need to show the *type* of difficulty which is being experienced in any particular instance.

Understanding the learning process
Although learning is a complex activity, psychologists have shown that it can be broken down, and understood, as consisting of a number of simple stages. We are going to describe these with the aid of a diagram. Whenever learning takes

place, these are essentially the stages involved. Thus the diagram describes how *each* of us learns – it can provide a useful check for discovering just where the 'block' is occurring when an individual is experiencing a learning difficulty. We believe that it is possible, in any instance, to 'diagnose' the type of learning difficulty before 'prescribing' the type of help the teacher can give.

In addition to the diagram, we summarise the steps as a series of questions which the teacher should ask himself in logical sequence. We expect that some of you may wish to return to this part of the book if you should meet with a particularly tricky problem at any stage during the design and application of a teaching programme. It should be stressed that the diagram, and the accompanying questions, serve only to help you discover the *kind* of difficulty concerned. It tells us nothing about the underlying cause or reason for the difficulty.

In Figure 2, the learner is represented by the large box, divided into sections, and the task is represented by the small box. The learner and the task may be seen as forming a 'loop.' To the left of the diagram we see several arrows trying to enter the system. We may regard these as distractors – only the information which is relevant to the task should be attended to. Already we can see the usefulness of this approach. If there are too many competing distractors – if the noise level of the room, or the variety of visual experiences present, are too great – then the learner will find it relatively more difficult to attend to the task.

Let us now look within the learner himself. We see that information may enter through the various senses. We know that it is stored for a very brief period in order to allow the individual to select what to attend to. But how does he know what this should be? Looking further into the diagram we see an arrow coming from the box labelled 'decision making'. This itself is linked to a box labelled 'permanent memory'. In other words, the learner decides what he must

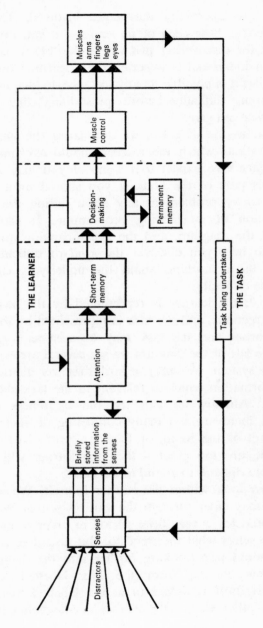

Figure 2. A diagram showing the way in which a person interacts with a task being carried out.

attend to on the basis of his previous experience. Clearly, in the early stages of learning any task, he will not have such previous experience to rely upon. It is at this stage, as we will see later, that he will need some help.

Let us assume, for now, that the learner attends to the correct part of the task. The message then passes through the box labelled 'short-term memory'. This stores it just long enough to enable him to decide what to do with it. An example of this is when you look up a number in a telephone directory, and recite it to yourself whilst fumbling for that elusive 2p coin before you dial. In this example, we see that the decision to dial the number is followed by the act of dialling. Decisions lead to actions, and in our diagram we show this by an arrow pointing to the box labelled 'muscle control'.

If the process has so far been concerned with acquiring the information necessary for the task, then the action which results will be the next step in the task itself, the results of which will be new information for the learner to attend to. This is what we mean by a loop.

Let us first consider the performance of an experienced person. We will take a familiar example, that of a dart player in a noisy, crowded pub. He stands at the appropriate distance from the dart board, dart in hand, ready to throw. In the background there is a great deal of noise. The babble of conversation, occasional laughter, sounds of clinking glass. People are continually moving to the left and right of him and the smell of tobacco smoke fills the air. He throws his first dart, double twenty. A pause, he has calculated that he would now only need double four to win. His eyes search for it, he readjusts his stance, and throws. We can fit this into the diagram.

Let us look at the stages involved: against the background of competing distractors he kept his eyes fixed on the dart board. More precisely, he gazed intently at the double twenty. He took careful aim. At this moment his previous

B

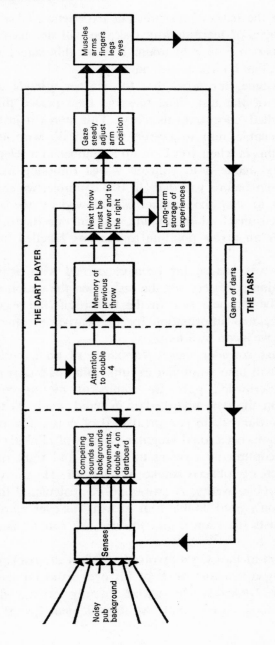

Figure 3. A diagram showing the way in which a dart player's skilled performance may be examined.

experience in years of dart playing helped him to adjust his throw – double twenty. The cheers slightly distracted him and he looked round, seeking quiet. He had previously calculated that if he obtained 'double top', he would need double four to win. His arm returned to the same position as on the previous throw, and as the memory of that still seemed to be present in his arm joint, he aimed slightly to the right and softened his throw. The dart dropped that $2\frac{1}{2}$ inches lower – firmly into the double four.

Here we can see the complete cycle, illustrated in the diagram. The experience of the previous throw has helped the player to make the necessary adjustment for his second throw. If he had been distracted, especially by a sudden movement seen from the corner of his eye, he might have misthrown.

Looking back at the diagram, you will see that the large box, representing the 'learner', is divided up by dotted lines. This is to show that the learning process consists of a number of stages, difficulty with any of which could result in failure to complete the task. We may regard the overall space within the box as representing an individual's 'capacity' to perform. We have just used the example of a dart player, now let us consider the case of someone learning to drive a car. We will assume that the car has a manual gear box. In this example we see that some parts of the task require more 'capacity' than do others, especially for a learner!

The learner sits in the driving seat, adjusting the position of the seat, the angle of the mirror, and fastening the seat belt. The instructor says: 'Today we are going to practise pulling smoothly into the traffic and making left-hand turns.' At this point, how many of you remember thinking 'I'll never remember all this'. Remember checking that the hand brake is on, and the gear lever in the neutral position, depressing the clutch with the left foot whilst pushing the gear lever into first position, revving with the right foot. 'Don't over-rev, ease up on the clutch pedal with your left foot until you find that point of contact. Now signal that you are going to pull out, check your mirror, look over your right shoulder, good, now, gently let off the hand brake . . .' At this point your left foot seems to jerk involuntarily and with a jolt the engine stops – you have stalled it, and have to go through the process all over again.

The diagram should help us to understand what is happening. So many signals need to be attended to, the muscular sensations telling us of the position of our feet, the sound of the engine, the instructor's voice, and so on, all this against the background of the roar of passing traffic. It is difficult to *select which of these incoming stimuli to attend to* at any one time. Quite clearly our performance can become 'blocked' at this point. If we do manage to achieve that 'point of contact', and prevent the revs from roaring away, then we can easily fail at the next stage – we *may forget* the correct sequence to be followed when checking the mirror, signalling, looking over the right shoulder, and releasing the hand brake.

Even if we do achieve all this successfully, we are painfully aware of the *difficulty of deciding* just *when* to pull out into that stream of traffic. Not only our life but that of our instructor is at stake! Once we have pulled out and are chugging along in first gear, we become aware of the *difficulty in controlling and coordinating* our movements. 'Do not over steer, don't transfer movement to the steering wheel whilst changing gear with the left hand, brake – gently', and so on. How we envy the apparently automatic performance of an experienced driver.

We can now see one of the most exciting results of our efforts to learn – the more we practise performing the correct movements, the easier they become. What originally took all our concentration now requires less. The learner driver found at first that the task took up all his available 'capacity' (see the diagram). With practice, however, certain operations become smoother, more automatic. There is some spare capacity and he can more easily attend to, even anticipate, what the instructor is saying. Indeed, experienced drivers can enjoy the scenery, listen to the radio, and hold a conversation all at the same time.

The person with 'learning difficulty'

If we now consider a person who has difficulty in learning, we find that the same process takes place. Learning may take longer and may need to be broken up into more stages. It is certain, however, that if he succeeds in mastering the task, then his performance will subsequently become easier and easier. His greater efficiency in carrying out the task will mean that he has some spare capacity. It is important that this should be realised. Once a mentally handicapped person has learned a task very well, he sometimes finds himself rated as 'inattentive', or 'distractible'. This is simply because *without any worsening in performance,* he now needs to attend to the task less. This may be a good indication that he should move on to learn something new, or more demanding.

Some research has been carried out into the difficulties experienced by mentally handicapped people when learning what to attend to. If asked to select from a number of objects of different colours and shapes, they often have an initial difficulty in knowing which of these features to attend to. But once they have learned that the correct object differs from the others in its colour, say, they quickly learn to choose the red one or the blue one. Much success has been achieved by paying particular attention to such difficulty, and exaggerating the important feature in the early stages of learning, as for example by using an exceptionally bright colour.

Other research has focussed on the problem faced by many mentally handicapped people in remembering things. In particular, that part of the memory known as 'immediate' memory, which stores information for very short periods, appears to need some help. This help might mean presenting the signal or information more clearly and slowly, or appealing to more than one sense at the same time: using a visual and an aural signal at once, perhaps. Repetition, soon afterwards, has also proved effective. It was widely agreed by such researchers, on the other hand, that once material *had* been learned by handicapped people, it was remembered very well indeed.

Some research has been concerned also with the ability to abstract general principles from various experiences. Although this has proved to present difficulties to many mentally handicapped people, it has been found that much progress can be made by careful training. For example, once they have been taught to place items into categories, such as clothing, tools, animals, many individuals can use the categories to recall many more items when a long list containing such items has been read to them.

There have been many other examples of research exploring how learning may be transferred to a new situation and successfully applied. It has involved not only abstract ideas and concepts, such as categories of things, but also the way in which problems may be approached and solved, and the ability to transfer manual skills, for example, from one complex task to another. A general conclusion must be that the basic learning process experienced by mentally handicapped people is the same as that which we all experience. The same basic stages are involved, as shown in the diagram on page 32. Indeed, by studying the particular difficulties which many of them experience, we have learned a great deal more about the way in which we all learn.

By considering the above research findings in relation to the diagram, you should now have a clearer idea of what is meant by 'learning difficulty'. Any complex task presents the learner with a sequence of different problems to overcome. If your son or daughter has difficulty in learning a new task, you should now be starting to ask what kind of problem is it – at what stage is he or she getting stuck? The whole of the previous section, including the various parts of the diagram, may now be summed up by a set of questions, to be asked in logical order. As you will see, only if the answer to any question is 'yes', should you move on to the next question. If, on the other hand, the answer is 'no', then you have found the problem. Of course, when this problem has been overcome you may find that other problems occur later in the sequence.

Thus, a person described as a 'slow learner' may be experiencing one or more of a number of different types of difficulty. Fortunately, no one is likely to experience *all* of them! Some individuals will find difficulties in attending, in choosing between alternatives, in remembering what to do next, in being able to initiate the action without prompting, or even difficulty with the performance of the action in a controlled manner. In any given task, because each task is different, the type and severity of difficulty experienced will probably provide a unique challenge to the learner. Fortunately, however, *whenever* learning difficulty is detected the same systematic series of questions may be applied. They are presented in the next section.

Discovering the Type of Learning Difficulty

Whenever a learning 'block' occurs, the following check may be carried out.

1. Is the learner comfortable and at ease? For instance, he may be hungry, needing a toilet, showing signs of apprehension.
2. Is he awake and alert? (The time of day is important here, and remember that some forms of medication may produce drowsiness.)
3. Has the whole task been demonstrated to him? (He may have stopped because he lacks the concept of the end product.)

4. Does he *want* to learn to carry out the task? (Once we are sure that he knows what is involved, we should ask him how he feels about the task.)

These are obvious preliminary checks. If you can answer 'yes' to them all, allow him to try the task again, and at the first appearance of difficulty, ask these further questions:

5. Is he able to see and hear what is required in the task? (If 'no', he may need to wear spectacles or a hearing aid.)

6. Have you ensured that the background noise is not too loud and that there are not too many visual distractors? (Even if his hearing and vision are perfect, too many competing stimuli mean that his senses are being bombarded.)

7. Is he attending to the correct feature relevant to this stage of the task? (If you say 'Take it in your right hand' – does he know which hand this is?)

8. Does he remember what to do next? (Check this by asking him – the demonstration he received may have been too long ago. The more stages there are in a task, the more difficult it is to remember them in the correct order.)

9. Will he carry out the next part of the task without being prompted? (He may know what to do next but be waiting for you to nod, smile, or say 'Go ahead'.)

10. Can he perform the actual operation required? (If a difficult manipulation is involved, he may hesitate prior to reaching this point in order to avoid failure.)

We hope that you will find the questions included in this section, together with the previous diagram, a useful basis for your understanding of the teaching principles to be described in Chapter 6. Although these principles will be seen to operate in any good teaching situation, they are particularly powerful when applied by one who has a basic understanding of the type of difficulty which a learner may be experiencing.

When someone 'fails' to learn something, then one of three things can happen. He can be taken off a task, usually to be given something less demanding to do; he can be provided with an aid, or a 'jig', which enables him to carry out the task but not to overcome his problem; or he may be subjected to systematic teaching which includes attention to the particular difficulty. All too often in the past, the first of these alternatives has been chosen. The danger is that this leads to a self-fulfilling prophecy – because the individual has 'failed', opportunities to try are restricted, the individual becomes bored, or develops a 'behaviour problem', and even simpler tasks are assumed to be beyond him. The negative behaviours shown are regarded as proof that the original task was a traumatic experience and that learning difficulty is severe!

In taking a more positive view, we intend to ensure that you are realistic. We have found that some parents of handicapped people sometimes become over optimistic about what may be achieved following early successes, whilst other parents appear to be unduly pessimistic. Research in this field is extensive, and world-wide. Many studies have illustrated the difficulties which mentally handicapped individuals have with various aspects of the learning process. Once the difficulties have been overcome, however, research shows that their memory is usually excellent.

Some exciting recent research has been concerned not simply with whether or not an individual can learn something, but with how he is able to cope with new situations. Colleagues from the Elwyn Institute in Pennsylvania have been studying the phenomena of 'helplessness' and 'acquiescence'.

'Helplessness' describes the state in which some individuals find themselves after a prolonged period when most important decisions have been taken for them – when the

B*

necessities of life have been provided with little effort required on their part. Individuals who have spent long periods living in institutions often develop a characteristic passivity. They are unable to perform an independent action, often showing fewer signs of exploratory behaviour, of searching for solutions to everyday problems. They cannot cope with novel situations, such as emergencies, or the appearance of a stranger. In extreme cases, they may become withdrawn and non-communicative.

The term 'acquiescence' is used to describe the submissive, or gullible, behaviour of many mentally handicapped people. In recent years research has focussed on the causes of such behaviour, linking it very strongly to the conditions and circumstances which may have led to it. In particular, parental attitudes, the stifling form of care provided in some residential and day facilities, and society's prevailing value system have been implicated.

It is clearly important for an ordered society that individuals should conform, in general, to the rules of behaviour, as well as to the law, which prevail in that culture. Individuals who have difficulty in learning, particularly in learning abstract concepts, need to be given special educational help in such areas. It is possible to teach an individual when to submit to authority, and how to recognise situations where such authority does not exist, or when submission would be inappropriate. Most of us learn such things incidentally, as a result of everyday experience. You may wish to devise some exercises to help your son or daughter to be less acquiescent or less submissive.

3 Assessing coping behaviour

When we refer to 'assessment' in this book, we are essentially concerned with the measurement of behaviour. Before you can choose your goal and embark upon any programme of training, you need to know a good deal about how your son or daughter is coping at present. In this Chapter you are given the means of assessing your own son or daughter – of checking whether certain kinds of behaviour occur or not.

If it is made too complicated or time consuming, we have found that assessment tends to become an end in itself. In order to avoid this, and to stress the close link between assessment and training, we are providing you with a special chart which can easily be completed, simply by ticking the appropriate box. You can carry out this form of assessment quite reliably. In fact, it is much more useful than depending solely upon psychological tests, such as tests of intelligence, which are often given on only one or two occasions.

It is now becoming more accepted that the parent has an important role to play in assessment, as well as in training. Whether the handicapped individual concerned is at school or at training centre during the day, this will account only for approximately one-third of the day. It is clearly important that assessment should include attention not only to what happens during these hours but also to what happens within the home or living environment. One important reason for involving parents, therefore, is to enable a check to be carried out concerning whether abilities acquired at school or at training centre are being put to use in the home, or vice-versa.

The basis of any assessment must be observation. Clearly, those who are with the individual for a good deal of time have the best opportunity to make observations. One of the greatest difficulties to be faced, however, is deciding what to include. Of all the behaviours which take place during the day, which are significant and worthy of note? The process should not be left to chance, it is too important for this. A further difficulty is that the closeness to an individual often itself leads one to overlook important aspects of behaviour. Both parents and staff have admitted that they grow accustomed to the mannerisms, speech, and varying moods of handicapped individuals, and so tend to 'see' what they have come to expect. Unconsciously, they may adjust their own behaviour accordingly, and find it difficult to stand back and examine the behaviour afresh.

Reliable observation is a skill which must be acquired through practice. We have to try to become more objective, to look carefully and avoid jumping to conclusions before they are justified. A good exercise is to compare your own observations with those of someone else who has had the same opportunity to observe a particular event. You may be surprised to discover how difficult it is to achieve complete agreement. It is well known that witnesses to a car accident frequently give very different versions of what happened.

At this stage, we suggest a short exercise in observing. Mum and Dad both watch a short television sequence – the national news, for example. Observe the behaviour of the newscaster. Agree to count the number of times a particular piece of behaviour occurs: how often he/she looks down, raises his/her eyebrows, blinks, or smiles. Compare your totals afterwards. Then ask each other questions about the newscaster's hair style, style of dress, for example. Note how much more difficult it is to agree on something you were not looking for in advance! Incidentally, can either of you recall the main items of the news? In concentrating on the newscaster's appearance you will probably have missed a good deal of *what* was actually said.

It is to take account of some of these difficulties, that we are providing you with a scale for assessing your son's or daughter's level of coping behaviour. By reading through the chart you will become familiar in advance with the items of behaviour to look for. It will thus help to sharpen your skills of observation. The chart, which may be completed in pencil, also enables you to record your assessment so that changes may be noted at a later date. We describe other forms of recording, related to specific teaching plans, in more detail in Chapter 7.

It would not be possible to include in detail *all* the items of behaviour which research has shown to be important for independent functioning in the community. Clearly, this would require a complete listing of all the items included in all published scales of individual development, from birth to adulthood! In this book we are concerned with a particular stage of development, the adolescent stage. Although we know that later, more adult behaviours, build upon the abilities first developed as babies or young children, we must assume that much of this early development has already taken place. Other books in this series focus on the development of handicapped babies and children and they list scales which are of use for assessing these earlier stages of development. In choosing items to include in the scale which you are to complete, we have been selective. We have chosen items of behaviour which numerous research studies have shown to be particularly important if an individual is to cope successfully in the community. The larger range of relevant items out of which the scale items have been selected are presented, for your information, in Table 2.

Table 2. Areas which are important for coping

Self-help

| Use of toilet | Hygiene |
| use of public toilets | washing face, hands, hair, |

bathing, use of deodorants, brushing teeth, shaving, menstruation
Grooming
combing hair
Appearance
Selection of clothing
Dressing/undressing
Care of clothing
ironing, pressing, repairing, laundering
Simple cooking
snacks, meals, beverages
Setting and clearing table
eating and drinking, use of cutlery
Table habits
Washing up
Making bed

Tidying room
Leisure at home
First aid/health
handling emergencies, taking medication, contacting doctor, attention to diet, recognising danger
Community knowledge
where to seek help, advice, use of Post Office, bank
Public transport
Shopping
recognising types of shops, making purchases
Eating out
Housework
knowledge and use of household appliances, tools, cleaning materials, etc.

Social Academic

Communication
prelanguage skills e.g. use of gesture, talk in sentences, understanding language, clarity of pronunciation
Reading
social sight vocabulary
Writing
completing simple forms, writing letters, signature
Recognition of number
Use of number
counting, measuring, weighing, simple arithmetic

Telling time
Concept of time
time estimation, seasons, age, passage of time, days, month, calendar
Money
coin and note recognition, knowledge of values, coin equivalents
Use of money
making purchases, budgeting, savings
Colour recognition
discrimination between colours, colour association,

e.g. traffic lights
Telephone
  answering the telephone, making calls from domestic telephone, public call box
Shape recognition
Knowledge of current affairs
Knowledge of surroundings, town, city, etc.

Interpersonal

Personal knowledge
  self-awareness
Conversation
  initiating a conversation, holding a conversation, asking for help, use of telephone
Social graces
  manners, courtesy, social give and take
Friendships
  consideration for others, awareness of others
Leisure
  group membership

Responsibility
Handling problems
Socially acceptable behaviour
Sexual knowledge
Sexual behaviour
Preparation for marriage
Expressing opinions
Mannerisms
Posture
Concern for others
Helping others
Self-concept
Ability to discriminate between situations

Vocational

Dexterity
Speed
Punctuality
Time keeping
Attendance
Consistency of performance
Adaptability
Accuracy
Quality
Knowledge of tools
Care of tools

Amount of supervision
Response to supervision
Relationship with co-workers
Checks own work
Level of task
Safety
Exercising foresight and initiative
Comprehension
Emotional stability
Decision making

Concentration
Working under pressure
Personal appearance
Hygiene
Self-confidence
Responsibility
Following rules and regulations
Understand work terms
Understand pay packet
Job search skills, e.g. how to
look for a job
Filling in application forms
Behaviour at interview
Use of machinery
Attention to task
Attitude to task
Creativity
Leadership
Measuring
Counting

As you can see, the items in the table are grouped under four headings. These are the principal areas of any curriculum of training which aims to develop independent skills. The headings are: Self-help, Social Academic, Interpersonal, and Vocational. Chapters 8, 9 and 10 respectively, deal with the first three of these headings. In these chapters we present exercises around which you can develop teaching plans as described in Chapter 6.

Although we recognise the importance of vocational exploration and training, it is too large a subject to be dealt with in a single chapter, deserving a book to itself at a later date.

Before presenting the scale itself, we want to be sure that you are clear about what it will help you to achieve. In designing the scale, we have tried to take account of your need to make quick and appropriate decisions about what you might go on to do. We ask you to consider a series of key questions, each logically related to the others, concerning each of the behaviours listed in the scale. It is not enough to know whether your son or daughter can do a particular thing. You need to know whether he or she can do it with or without help and whether abilities are being put to proper use. You must then be able to decide where further assessment or training is required, and discover where opportunities exist and where they may be lacking. The following diagram, in the form of a flow-chart, shows these questions arranged in a logical sequence, and the type of action which different answers suggest may be necessary.

As you can see from the diagram the sequence of questions is:

1. Can he do it without help? There may be three possible answers to this. If the answer is 'uncertain', then it will be necessary to let him try this and observe his attempts. If the answer is 'No', then we should ask question 2. If the answer is 'Yes' proceed to question 3.
2. Can he do it with help? If the answer to this is still 'No' then clearly a training programme is necessary. If the answer to this question is 'Yes' then training may be necessary to enable him to perform it without help.
3. The next logical question is 'Does he do it an adequate amount? Again three answers are possible. If the answer is 'Uncertain', then it is possible that you feel that you do not have an adequate yardstick and so you should discuss this behaviour with other parents, or with the teacher or instructor. If the answer is 'Yes' then we can assume that this ability is not only present but is being adequately put to use. If the answer is 'No' we may then ask a further question.
4. Does he do it at all? If the answer to this is 'Yes', implying that the behaviour is not shown often enough, then he may need enouragement – some suitable rewards – if he is to put the ability to proper use. If the answer to the question is 'No' then a further question should be asked.
5. Is there opportunity for the behaviour to be shown? Of most interest here would be the response 'No'. This will mean that opportunities should be created.

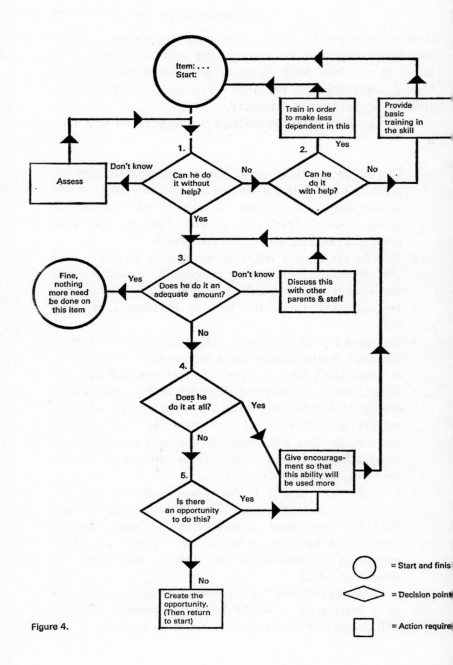

Figure 4.

In short, depending on what action you have ticked for particular areas of ability, different courses of action will be needed. You must either carry out further assessment, design and apply a programme of training, select more effective rewards, or begin by creating the necessary opportunities.

You should now turn to the Scale for Assessing Coping Skills which is presented in the following pages. We suggest that, where possible, Mum and Dad should work together in carrying out this assessment. Even if you own this book, we suggest that you complete the scale using a pencil.

The Scale for Assessing Coping Skills
Read through the whole scale first in order to get an idea of the areas it covers and the kind of questions it is asking. You will see that the items are grouped under headings, and within each group there is a gradual progression in the difficulty of the items concerned. The scale should be completed by ticking the appropriate box (or boxes) which apply to each in turn.

The layout of the scale makes it possible for you to see, at a glance, what the present position is and what type of thing needs to be done in order to make progress. For example, if you are able to tick both columns 1 and 5 for a particular item, such as eating with a knife, fork or spoon, then you are saying that your youngster can do this without help and is using this ability appropriately. This is fine – you have just pinpointed one of your youngster's strengths. We will come back to this later, but for now it means there is nothing you need to do about it – so move on to the next item. You may find, however, that although some items are ticked under the column 1 they are also ticked under column 6 – in other words, although a certain skill is present, not enough use is being made of it. You must try to discover why – maybe he or she needs some encouragement.

(*continued on page 70*)

SELF HELP (Personal)

1. Selection of clothing

ITEM	1 Can do without help or supervision	2 Can do but only with help or supervision	3 Cannot yet do	4 Do not yet know whether he can do	5 Uses this ability an adequate amount	6 Does not use this an adequate amount	7 There is no opportunity to do this
(a) Selects own clothes from drawer or wardrobe	☐	☐	☐	☐	☐	☐	☐
(b) Chooses clothing and footwear suitable for weather conditions	☐	☐	☐	☐	☐	☐	☐
(c) Chooses clothing and footwear appropriate to occasion (e.g. work, party)	☐	☐	☐	☐	☐	☐	☐
(d) Shows personal preferences and awareness of fashion	☐	☐	☐	☐	☐	☐	☐
(e) Locates clothing/footwear shops or departments and knows own sizes	☐	☐	☐	☐	☐	☐	☐

2. Undressing/dressing

ITEM	1	2	3	4	5	6	7
(a) Removes simple articles of clothing (e.g. socks, underwear)	☐	☐	☐	☐	☐	☐	☐
(b) Puts on simple articles of clothing	☐	☐	☐	☐	☐	☐	☐
(c) Removes garments requiring unbuttoning or unzipping	☐	☐	☐	☐	☐	☐	☐
(d) Puts on garments requiring buttoning, zipping, tying	☐	☐	☐	☐	☐	☐	☐
(e) Completely dresses self, in sensible sequence (e.g. does not put shoes on before socks)	☐	☐	☐	☐	☐	☐	☐

ITEM	1 Can do without help or super-vision	2 Can do but only with help or supervision	3 Cannot yet do	4 Do not yet know whether he can do	5 Uses this ability an adequate amount	6 Does not use this an adequate amount	7 There is no opportunity to do this
3. Use of toilet							
(a) Recognises when needing toilet	☐	☐	☐	☐	☐	☐	☐
(b) Uses toilet by self	☐	☐	☐	☐	☐	☐	☐
(c) Flushes toilet and adjusts dress	☐	☐	☐	☐	☐	☐	☐
(d) Keeps toilet clean, leaving fit for others to use. (Ladies: disposes of sanitary materials appropriately)	☐	☐	☐	☐	☐	☐	☐
(e) Uses public conveniences, knows difference between ladies and gents, can operate coin mechanism	☐	☐	☐	☐	☐	☐	☐
4. Personal hygiene							
(a) Washes hands and face when needed, after toilet, before meal	☐	☐	☐	☐	☐	☐	☐
(b) Takes bath or shower when needed. Uses deodorants	☐	☐	☐	☐	☐	☐	☐
(c) Cleans teeth properly	☐	☐	☐	☐	☐	☐	☐
(d) Washes hair properly	☐	☐	☐	☐	☐	☐	☐
(e) Changes underwear and socks regularly. (Ladies: Copes with menstruation appropriately)	☐	☐	☐	☐	☐	☐	☐

ITEM	1 Can do without help or supervision	2 Can do but only with help or supervision	3 Cannot yet do	4 Do not yet know whether he can do	5 Uses this ability an adequate amount	6 Does not use this an adequate amount	7 There is no opportunity to do this
5. Grooming and appearance							
(a) Cleans and cuts nails	☐	☐	☐	☐	☐	☐	☐
(b) Blows nose and uses handkerchief	☐	☐	☐	☐	☐	☐	☐
(c) Shaves (if necessary) (Ladies: under arms, and legs if necessary)	☐	☐	☐	☐	☐	☐	☐
(d) Combs or brushes hair	☐	☐	☐	☐	☐	☐	☐
(e) Visits barbers/hairdressers	☐	☐	☐	☐	☐	☐	☐
SELF HELP (domestic)							
6. Care of clothing							
(a) Puts clothes away, hangs them up	☐	☐	☐	☐	☐	☐	☐
(b) Cleans and polishes shoes	☐	☐	☐	☐	☐	☐	☐
(c) Knows when clothes need laundering/dry cleaning	☐	☐	☐	☐	☐	☐	☐
(d) Irons simple articles	☐	☐	☐	☐	☐	☐	☐
(e) Carries out simple repairs, stitching on patch, buttons, etc.	☐	☐	☐	☐	☐	☐	☐

ITEM	1 Can do without help or supervision	2 Can do but only with help or supervision	3 Cannot yet do	4 Do not yet know whether he can do	5 Uses this ability an adequate amount	6 Does not use this an adequate amount	7 There is no opportunity to do this
7. Food and drink preparation							
(a) Makes hot drinks	☐	☐	☐	☐	☐	☐	☐
(b) Can assemble ingredients, open tins, packets, or bottles	☐	☐	☐	☐	☐	☐	☐
(c) Prepares vegetables for cooking, shells peas, peel potatoes	☐	☐	☐	☐	☐	☐	☐
(d) Follows simple recipe or instructions	☐	☐	☐	☐	☐	☐	☐
(e) Selects correct oven temperature and monitors cooking	☐	☐	☐	☐	☐	☐	☐
8. Setting (and clearing) table							
(a) Places mat, salt and pepper etc.	☐	☐	☐	☐	☐	☐	☐
(b) Sets simple place: correctly positions knife, fork, spoon, glass	☐	☐	☐	☐	☐	☐	☐
(c) Places serving dishes and serving utensils	☐	☐	☐	☐	☐	☐	☐
(d) Clears away, taking care with breakables	☐	☐	☐	☐	☐	☐	☐
(e) Clears cloth, shakes, wipes down table	☐	☐	☐	☐	☐	☐	☐

ITEM	1 Can do without help or supervision	2 Can do but only with help or supervision	3 Cannot yet do	4 Do not yet know whether he can do	5 Uses this ability an adequate amount	6 Does not use this an adequate amount	7 There is no opportunity to do this
9. Table habits							
(a) Uses knife, fork and spoon appropriately	☐	☐	☐	☐	☐	☐	☐
(b) Serves food and drink to self in reasonable quantity	☐	☐	☐	☐	☐	☐	☐
(c) Pours out liquids with care, no spilling	☐	☐	☐	☐	☐	☐	☐
(d) Considers others, passes salt, etc.	☐	☐	☐	☐	☐	☐	☐
(e) Eats unoffensively, mouth closed, no spilling, at correct speed	☐	☐		☐	☐	☐	☐
10. Washing up							
(a) Dries items and puts away	☐	☐	☐	☐	☐	☐	☐
(b) Prepares dishes for washing, clearing food scraps into bin	☐	☐	☐	☐	☐	☐	☐
(c) Prepares bowl or sink, correct water temperature and amount of washing up liquid	☐	☐	☐	☐	☐	☐	☐
(d) Washes greasy dishes thoroughly, top and bottom, no breakages	☐	☐	☐	☐	☐	☐	☐
(e) Washes cups, saucers, cutlery and glassware, taking care	☐	☐	☐	☐	☐	☐	☐

ITEM	Can do without help or supervision	Can do but only with help or supervision	Cannot yet do	Do not yet know whether he can do	Uses this ability an adequate amount	Does not use this an adequate amount	There is no opportunity to do this
11. Making the bed							
(a) Strips bed down	☐	☐	☐	☐	☐	☐	☐
(b) Puts pillowcases on pillows	☐	☐	☐	☐	☐	☐	☐
(c) Tucks bedclothes in at sides	☐	☐	☐	☐	☐	☐	☐
(d) Puts bedclothes on in right order	☐	☐	☐	☐	☐	☐	☐
(e) Pulls sheets straight, avoids wrinkles in bed	☐	☐	☐	☐	☐	☐	☐
12. Tidying room							
(a) Tidies things away in proper place, games in cupboard, books on shelf etc.	☐	☐	☐	☐	☐	☐	☐
(b) Dusts surfaces	☐	☐	☐	☐	☐	☐	☐
(c) Sweeps/vacuums carpet, also under the bed	☐	☐	☐	☐	☐	☐	☐
(d) Cleans window(s) and mirror(s)	☐	☐	☐	☐	☐	☐	☐
(e) Decorates walls, reflecting personal interests (posters, certificates, beer mats, etc.)	☐	☐	☐	☐	☐	☐	☐

ITEM	1 Can do without help or super-vision	2 Can do but only with help or supervision	3 Cannot yet do	4 Do not yet know whether he can do	5 Uses this ability an adequate amount	6 Does not use this an adequate amount	7 There is no opportunity to do this
13. Leisure at home							
(a) Decides how to spend own time	☐	☐	☐	☐	☐	☐	☐
(b) Occupies self for short periods	☐	☐	☐	☐	☐	☐	☐
(c) Selects favourite TV or radio pro-gramme(s)	☐	☐	☐	☐	☐	☐	☐
(d) Plays indoor games, dominoes, cards, table-tennis, etc.	☐	☐	☐	☐	☐	☐	☐
(e) Engages in a creative hobby or interest	☐	☐	☐	☐	☐	☐	☐
14. First aid and health							
(a) Shows awareness of danger and exercises caution	☐	☐	☐	☐	☐	☐	☐
(b) Knows how to obtain appropriate help in emergency, fire-brigade, police, ambulance	☐	☐	☐	☐	☐	☐	☐
(c) Treats simple injuries, and minor ailments, cuts, headaches	☐	☐	☐	☐	☐	☐	☐
(d) Takes simple health precautions, chang-ing wet clothes, attention to weight	☐	☐	☐	☐	☐	☐	☐
(e) Seeks medical help when required and takes medicine reliably	☐	☐	☐	☐	☐	☐	☐

SELF HELP (community)
15. Community knowledge

ITEM	1 Can do without help or super-vision	2 Can do but only with help or supervision	3 Cannot yet do	4 Do not yet know whether he can do	5 Uses this ability an adequate amount	6 Does not use this an adequate amount	7 There is no opportunity to do this
(a) Can find own street and house, knows name and number	☐	☐	☐	☐	☐	☐	☐
(b) Knows neighbourhood and can find way around	☐	☐	☐	☐	☐	☐	☐
(c) Observes safety rules when crossing road	☐	☐	☐	☐	☐	☐	☐
(d) Knows location and function of community services, shops, Post Office, bank, library etc.	☐	☐	☐	☐	☐	☐	☐
(e) Ask directions and knows what to do if lost	☐	☐	☐	☐	☐	☐	☐

16. Local transport

ITEM	1	2	3	4	5	6	7
(a) Recognises correct bus stop and bus number for intended journey	☐	☐	☐	☐	☐	☐	☐
(b) Can state destination and pay fare	☐	☐	☐	☐	☐	☐	☐
(c) Alights at correct stop	☐	☐	☐	☐	☐	☐	☐
(d) Travels alone on the bus behaving appropriately	☐	☐	☐	☐	☐	☐	☐
(e) Can plan a bus journey to a place never previously visited by bus	☐	☐	☐	☐	☐	☐	☐

ITEM	1 Can do without help or supervision	2 Can do but only with help or supervision	3 Cannot yet do	4 Do not yet know whether he can do	5 Uses this ability an adequate amount	6 Does not use this an adequate amount	7 There is no opportunity to do this
17. Shopping							
(a) Goes errand with note or shopping list	☐	☐	☐	☐	☐	☐	☐
(b) Locates items, or asks assistant for help	☐	☐	☐	☐	☐	☐	☐
(c) Recognises difference between self service and other shops, behaves and pays appropriately	☐	☐	☐	☐	☐	☐	☐
(d) Shops for regular items, e.g. groceries, comparing prices	☐	☐	☐	☐	☐	☐	☐
(e) Shops for personal items, e.g. clothing, checking sizes, style, etc.	☐	☐	☐	☐	☐	☐	☐
18. Eating out							
(a) Knows difference between self-service and waiter service cafe or restaurant	☐	☐	☐	☐	☐	☐	☐
(b) Selects meal and drink and takes tray, cutlery etc., as required (in self-service cafe)	☐	☐	☐	☐	☐	☐	☐
(c) Orders from a menu, keeping to meals which can be afforded	☐	☐	☐	☐	☐	☐	☐
(d) Observes table habits acceptable to public eating	☐	☐	☐	☐	☐	☐	☐
(e) Locates pay-desk, or pays waiter. Avoids overtipping	☐	☐	☐	☐	☐	☐	☐

SOCIAL ACADEMIC
19. Communication

ITEM	Can do without help or supervision	Can do but only with help or supervision	Cannot yet do	Do not yet know whether he can do	Uses this ability an adequate amount	Does not use this an adequate amount	There is no opportunity to do this
(a) Makes wants known by gesture or language	☐	☐	☐	☐	☐	☐	☐
(b) Can say own name and address	☐	☐	☐	☐	☐	☐	☐
(c) Follows spoken instructions	☐	☐	☐	☐	☐	☐	☐
(d) Uses whole sentences, speaking clearly and distinctly	☐	☐	☐	☐	☐	☐	☐
(e) Explains feelings so that others can understand	☐	☐	☐	☐	☐	☐	☐

20. Reading

ITEM	Can do without help or supervision	Can do but only with help or supervision	Cannot yet do	Do not yet know whether he can do	Uses this ability an adequate amount	Does not use this an adequate amount	There is no opportunity to do this
(a) Recognises letters of the alphabet	☐	☐	☐	☐	☐	☐	☐
(b) Reads important words, such as 'danger' 'exit' 'toilet'	☐	☐	☐	☐	☐	☐	☐
(c) Can 'sound out' new words, using knowledge of letter sounds	☐	☐	☐	☐	☐	☐	☐
(d) Reads with understanding, e.g. uses newspaper to get information	☐	☐	☐	☐	☐	☐	☐
(e) Reads books, magazines, etc. for pleasure	☐	☐	☐	☐	☐	☐	☐

ITEM	1 Can do without help or supervision	2 Can do but only with help or supervision	3 Cannot yet do	4 Do not yet know whether he can do	5 Uses this ability an adequate amount	6 Does not use this an adequate amount	7 There is no opportunity to do this
21. Writing							
(a) Writes signature	☐	☐	☐	☐	☐	☐	☐
(b) Prints name, age, address	☐	☐	☐	☐	☐	☐	☐
(c) Fills in printed forms, coupons, etc.	☐	☐	☐	☐	☐	☐	☐
(d) Writes simple sentences, when dictated	☐	☐	☐	☐	☐	☐	☐
(e) Writes letters or messages which are easily understood	☐	☐	☐	☐	☐	☐	☐
22. Number							
(a) Counts by rote up to 10	☐	☐	☐	☐	☐	☐	☐
(b) Recognises and names numbers 1 to 10	☐	☐	☐	☐	☐	☐	☐
(c) Counts by rote and recognises numbers between 10 and 50	☐	☐	☐	☐	☐	☐	☐
(d) Counts and recognises numbers with three or more digits	☐	☐	☐	☐	☐	☐	☐
(e) Recognises and names fractions and decimal parts, (e.g. $12\frac{1}{2}$p, 98.4 degrees)	☐	☐	☐	☐	☐	☐	☐

ITEM	Can do without help or supervision	Can do but only with help or supervision	Cannot yet do	Do not yet know whether he can do	Uses this ability an adequate amount	Does not use this an adequate amount	There is no opportunity to do this
23. Use of number							
(a) Has ordinal concept of number: knows which of two numbers is bigger	☐	☐	☐	☐	☐	☐	☐
(b) Can use number scale when measuring or weighing self or goods	☐	☐	☐	☐	☐	☐	☐
(c) Adds or subtracts single numbers	☐	☐	☐	☐	☐	☐	☐
(d) Adds or subtracts numbers with two or more digits	☐	☐	☐	☐	☐	☐	☐
(e) Can do simple multiplication and division	☐	☐	☐	☐	☐	☐	☐
24. Telling the time							
(a) Tells time to nearest hour, using clock or watch	☐	☐	☐	☐	☐	☐	☐
(b) Tells time to nearest ¼ hour	☐	☐	☐	☐	☐	☐	☐
(c) Tells time to nearest minute	☐	☐	☐	☐	☐	☐	☐
(d) Sets a clock, e.g. alarm clock, to a given time	☐	☐	☐	☐	☐	☐	☐
(e) Uses 24 hour system, e.g. in reading a time-table	☐	☐	☐	☐	☐	☐	☐

ITEM	1 Can do without help or super-vision	2 Can do but only with help or supervision	3 Cannot yet do	4 Do not yet know whether he can do	5 Uses this ability an adequate amount	6 Does not use this an adequate amount	7 There is no opportunity to do this
25. Concept of time							
(a) Knows days of week	☐	☐	☐	☐	☐	☐	☐
(b) Associates certain times, or intervals, with daily activities, e.g. rise at 8.0 a.m., lunch between 1.0 and 2.0 p.m.	☐	☐	☐	☐	☐	☐	☐
(c) Knows months of year and order of seasons	☐	☐	☐	☐	☐	☐	☐
(d) Can plan events in advance, using calendar or timetables	☐	☐	☐	☐	☐	☐	☐
(e) Estimates passage of time fairly well (e.g. ¼ hr. ago)	☐	☐	☐	☐	☐	☐	☐
26. Money							
(a) Recognises and names coins	☐	☐	☐	☐	☐	☐	☐
(b) Recognises and names notes: £1.00, £5.00, £10.00 and so on	☐	☐	☐	☐	☐	☐	☐
(c) Understands equivalence of coins (2 x 5p equals 10p)	☐	☐	☐	☐	☐	☐	☐
(d) Understands equivalence of coins and notes (2 x 50p equals £1)	☐	☐	☐	☐	☐	☐	☐
(e) Can add coins together to reach a speci-fied amount, and can check change	☐	☐	☐	☐	☐	☐	☐

ITEM	Can do without help or supervision	Can do but only with help or supervision	Cannot yet do	Do not yet know whether he can do	Uses this ability an adequate amount	Does not use this an adequate amount	There is no opportunity to do this
27. Use of money							
(a) Makes purchases with coins or notes and checks change	☐	☐	☐	☐	☐	☐	☐
(b) Offers reasonable amount of money, where possible, when purchasing an item (e.g. 10p, not a £5 note for a packet of chewing gum)	☐	☐	☐	☐	☐	☐	☐
(c) Compares prices on goods before purchase	☐	☐	☐	☐	☐	☐	☐
(d) Spends money without overspending, can follow a simple budget – avoids debt	☐	☐	☐	☐	☐	☐	☐
(e) Saves up for desired items (has bank account or post office savings account)	☐	☐	☐	☐	☐	☐	☐
28. Colour recognition and use							
(a) Can name and match primary colours (red, yellow, blue) and black and white	☐	☐	☐	☐	☐	☐	☐
(b) Can name and match secondary colours (orange, green, purple)	☐	☐	☐	☐	☐	☐	☐
(c) Can name and match intermediary shades (grey, pink)	☐	☐	☐	☐	☐	☐	☐
(d) Responds appropriately to colour signs, traffic lights, for example	☐	☐	☐	☐	☐	☐	☐
(e) Avoids colour schemes which clash (e.g. red and orange)	☐	☐	☐	☐	☐	☐	☐

ITEM	1 Can do without help or supervision	2 Can do but only with help or supervision	3 Cannot yet do	4 Do not yet know whether he can do	5 Uses this ability an adequate amount	6 Does not use this an adequate amount	7 There is no opportunity to do this
INTERPERSONAL							
29. Personal knowledge							
(a) Knows full name, address, sex	☐	☐	☐	☐	☐	☐	☐
(b) Knows age and birthday and telephone number (where appropriate)	☐	☐	☐	☐	☐	☐	☐
(c) Knows nationality, name of country and religion	☐	☐	☐	☐	☐	☐	☐
(d) Can name and describe members of immediate family	☐	☐	☐	☐	☐	☐	☐
(e) Has fairly realistic idea of own strengths and limitations	☐	☐	☐	☐	☐	☐	☐
30. Conversation							
(a) Uses basic social conversation, 'Hello', 'good morning', 'how are you', etc.	☐	☐	☐	☐	☐	☐	☐
(b) Relates experiences, recent events, etc.	☐	☐	☐	☐	☐	☐	☐
(c) Talks about subject of interest to person concerned	☐	☐	☐	☐	☐	☐	☐
(d) Seeks other person's advice or opinion	☐	☐	☐	☐	☐	☐	☐
(e) Knows when someone is getting bored and brings conversation to an end, or	☐	☐	☐	☐	☐	☐	☐

ITEM	Can do without help or super-vision	Can do but only with help or supervision	Cannot yet do	Do not yet know whether he can do	Uses this ability an adequate amount	Does not use this an adequate amount	There is no opportunity to do this
31. Social graces							
(a) Says 'please' and 'thank you'	☐	☐	☐	☐	☐	☐	☐
(b) Greets others in appropriate way	☐	☐	☐	☐	☐	☐	☐
(c) Takes turn, waits patiently	☐	☐	☐	☐	☐	☐	☐
(d) Knocks on doors before entering, or excuses self, where appropriate	☐	☐	☐	☐	☐	☐	☐
(e) Can take hint when someone wants to leave or wants privacy	☐	☐	☐	☐	☐	☐	☐
32. Friendships							
(a) Generally tries to get along with others	☐	☐	☐	☐	☐	☐	☐
(b) Shares or lends possessions with discretion	☐	☐	☐	☐	☐	☐	☐
(c) Shows warmth or affection, kindness and sympathy	☐	☐	☐	☐	☐	☐	☐
(d) Keeps in touch with friend, remembers birthday, etc.	☐	☐	☐	☐	☐	☐	☐
(e) Considers friends' feelings, offers help where possible	☐	☐	☐	☐	☐	☐	☐

ITEM	1 Can do without help or supervision	2 Can do but only with help or supervision	3 Cannot yet do	4 Do not yet know whether he can do	5 Uses this ability an adequate amount	6 Does not use this an adequate amount	7 There is no opportunity to do this
33. Leisure – group activities							
(a) Enjoys being in the company of others, going to party, dance or disco	☐	☐	☐	☐	☐	☐	☐
(b) Attends a club or social centre	☐	☐	☐	☐	☐	☐	☐
(c) Goes to cinema, theatre, sporting or athletic event	☐	☐	☐	☐	☐	☐	☐
(d) Takes part in team games	☐	☐	☐	☐	☐	☐	☐
(e) Takes part in drama, concert, amateur theatrical, band or choir	☐	☐	☐	☐	☐	☐	☐
34. Telephone							
(a) Answers phone and calls appropriate person or takes simple message	☐	☐	☐	☐	☐	☐	☐
(b) Answers phone and carries on simple conversation	☐	☐	☐	☐	☐	☐	☐
(c) Dials and obtains a required number (written down) and asks for person concerned, including emergency	☐	☐	☐	☐	☐	☐	☐
(d) Uses a call-box for well-known numbers	☐	☐	☐	☐	☐	☐	☐
(e) Uses a telephone directory with some success	☐	☐	☐	☐	☐	☐	☐

35. Responsibility

ITEM	Can do without help or super-vision	Can do but only with help or supervision	Cannot yet do	Do not yet know whether he can do	Uses this ability an adequate amount	Does not use this an adequate amount	There is no opportunity to do this
(a) Aware of rules and the need to keep them (safety, honesty, punctuality, hygiene, etc.).	☐	☐	☐	☐	☐	☐	☐
(b) Accepts criticism where appropriate	☐	☐	☐	☐	☐	☐	☐
(c) Anticipates the consequence of own actions	☐	☐	☐	☐	☐	☐	☐
(d) Accepts blame for own mistakes	☐	☐	☐	☐	☐	☐	☐
(e) Shows concern for the safety or welfare of others	☐	☐	☐	☐	☐	☐	☐

36. Sexual knowledge and behaviour

ITEM	Can do without help or super-vision	Can do but only with help or supervision	Cannot yet do	Do not yet know whether he can do	Uses this ability an adequate amount	Does not use this an adequate amount	There is no opportunity to do this
(a) Aware of differences between men and women	☐	☐	☐	☐	☐	☐	☐
(b) Understands own sexual development, pubic hair, breasts, etc.	☐	☐	☐	☐	☐	☐	☐
(c) Knows how babies are conceived and born, in context of love and marriage	☐	☐	☐	☐	☐	☐	☐
(d) Aware of birth control, dangers of venereal disease, etc.	☐	☐	☐	☐	☐	☐	☐
(e) Behaves with responsibility and respect in relations with opposite sex (not over affectionate, or promiscuous)	☐	☐		☐	☐	☐	☐

Items ticked under columns 2 or 3 mean that training is needed, either in order to develop the ability in the first place, or to enable the activity to be carried out without help.

You may find that a number of items are ticked under column 4 – this means that you need to carry out an assessment in this area as you are not yet sure whether or not he or she has the ability concerned. You may not yet have had an opportunity to discover this. So finding a tick in column 7 means that your *first* task is to create the opportunity which is necessary before any further progress can be made. If for example, you don't know whether your youngster can use a knife and fork, you might provide him or her with these at the next meal. Look at your own completed chart to spot further examples.

Now that you know how to interpret your assessment chart, you should have a good overall idea of the degree of dependence of your son or daughter, and also of the areas in which progress has already been made. In short you now know a good deal more about his or her 'needs' and 'strengths'. At a glance, you have the information you need to help you to plan a scheme of work which will lead to an improvement in his or her coping behaviour.

Let us now look at the ticks in the 'Do not yet know' column of your chart, which suggest that you should provide an opportunity for your son or daughter to try the activity in question. Suppose you have a tick in a self-help area: 'Washing the dishes'. Following an actual meal, having ensured that all the necessary materials are available, you could take your youngster into the dining area, point to the dirty plates on the table, and say 'Let's see how good you are at washing up.' Then take him or her into the kitchen, indicate the sink, and say: 'Everything that you need is over there – I'm going to watch to see how you get on.'

Points to look for
Does he or she carry all the plates and cutlery to the sink area before commencing washing up?
Is food still adhering to the plates scraped into the waste bin?
Is an appropriate amount of water, at the right temperature, run into the sink or bowl?
Is washing-up liquid used and in the correct quantity?
Are non-greasy items washed first?
Is a suitable cloth or plastic scrubber used when cleaning the dishes, on both sides, in the water?
Is appropriate use made of the draining board, plate rack, etc.?
Are dishes, cutlery, rinsed and dried before being put away in the correct place?
Is the dirty water emptied from the sink or bowl and the latter cleaned?

Only if all these stages could be carried out correctly, without help or prompting, should the item have been ticked under the first column. When this exercise was carried out recently in an Adult Training Centre, for example, two of the three trainees scraped the food particles into the washing up water; two used water at the wrong temperature, and all three forgot to use washing-up liquid. On the basis of this observation alone, column 3 should be ticked. If observed during supervision, however, a rating of 2 may have been given. With more experience at observing your son or daughter attempting to carry out the items included in the scale, you will become more confident about which column to tick.

Some parents may find it very difficult to judge whether an item should be credited under column 5 or not. As suggested in Chapter 1, you may wish to discuss this between yourselves, or with parents of other handicapped individuals of a similar age, before deciding what would be reasonable.

We urge you to use your judgement here – if you feel that your youngster *is* using a particular ability an adequate amount at the present time, you can always review this decision at a later date.

You may feel overwhelmed by the amount of information which you now possess, and like many parents whom we have known, you may be wondering where to start, how to set training priorities. In the next two chapters, we offer hints about how to set about this and how to assemble the necessary resources. We recommend that you study these two chapters thoroughly before turning to Chapter 6, which is concerned with *how* to teach.

4   Selecting a goal

Now that you have completed your assessment chart, you are ready to select a training goal. In the previous chapter, when helping you to interpret your chart, we chose washing up to illustrate what you could do in cases where further assessment was needed. We strongly recommend that assessment should be carried out for all items which were ticked in column 4 – we want you to be sure that you have a full picture of your son's or daughter's current abilities. The goals selected should build upon existing strengths and should also reflect a system of priorities related to more successful coping.

In this chapter we hope to indicate, with examples, how specific goals may be selected. The goal itself must be expressed in clear, unambiguous terms. Of course, you may wish to design a teaching plan to develop some area of knowledge or skill not included in this scale. Please feel free to do this, the scale is only there as a resource for you to use. You may find it helpful, however, to see how the various items in the scale are related to different levels of independent functioning in the community. Later in the chapter we group items together, suggesting which abilities need to be present, and used, for an individual to be considered capable of that particular level of independence. As a guide, we suggest the form of living accommodation appropriate to each level. Although at present your youngster is probably living at home with you, you may wish to discover what form of alternative accommodation would be suitable, following training in the future.

The key to success in applying the principles to be described in Chapter 6 is the close involvement of your son

c*

or daughter from the beginning. A major influence upon your selection of a goal must be that it is something he or she *wants* to learn. Discuss the proposed goal, and the advantages of achieving it. You should certainly attempt to relate the goal to your son's or daughter's existing interests – learning to use public transport, for example, could help your son to get to that football match when no one is able to accompany him.

Before choosing any goals, therefore, sit down with your son or daughter and go through the completed chart together. Explain what the ticks mean, and express your pride in the achievements they represent. Point out the areas where, with further help, he or she could do something unaided. Point out which abilities are missing and say 'would you like to be able to do that?' If the answer is 'Yes', say 'tell me more about it, what would you do, where would you go,' etc. You may find that this is a new experience for your son or daughter, who may not be too confident about making decisions, or expressing preferences, in this way. Let us consider this more fully in the next section, and see what may be done about it.

Involving the Mentally Handicapped Person in Decision-Making

One of the most important findings of research is that we all tend to underestimate what mentally handicapped individuals are capable of. For parents there is the added difficulty of overcoming habits of caring and supporting which were necessary during the period of childhood. It is normal, for example, for parents to make decisions on behalf of young children – to choose the clothes they will wear, for instance, both when these are being purchased and when dressing in the morning. It is quick and convenient for a mother to assemble the necessary clothes for the day at the foot of the bed, say, rather than to leave the child to make his or her own selection from the drawer. And there are many similar examples of decisions which must be made during the day. It is important once your son or daughter is past early childhood, to ask yourself whether each decision is one which the person should really be making for himself. In other words, it is possible that some real opportunities are being lost simply through carry-over of old habits.

You may recall, from the diagram in Chapter 2, that some people displaying an apparent learning difficulty simply lack the initiative to carry out an action. They'll wait until someone nods, or smiles, or says 'Go ahead'. One well-known research worker who actually played the part of a mentally handicapped person going for job interview, described the experience afterwards as follows:

> After just two days of having doors opened for me, and of people not talking to me, but about me in my presence, I felt my personality slipping away. I waited for others to open a door for me . . .

People who have had experience of life in an institution report that decision-making can become progressively less and less necessary as there is always someone else prepared to decide for one. Indeed, in some extreme cases even the decision to speak becomes too difficult, resulting in a form of mutism. In short, we learn about ourselves, and the world around us, from the way in which people behave towards us and from the consequences of our actions. So rather than do things *for* a handicapped son or daughter, look out for and encourage any occasion when he or she shows initiative, and make it clear that you welcome this.

We now know that the opportunity to choose is an important key to success in any task. After all, this ability to make choices is one of the distinguishing features of adult status, and it has consistently emerged as the aspiration of mentally handicapped young adults during our conversations with them. In order to help your son or daughter to become more actively involved in choosing the goal to work towards, we first need to find out if he or she is already sufficiently involved in decision-making, or not.

So consider the events of an ordinary day and try to pinpoint occasions when decisions are necessary. You will find that there are some events which do not arise from our own decisions – for example, the telephone rings, or there is an unexpected visitor, or it begins to rain. Although these events may require a response on our part, they did not occur as a result of any decision that we made. On the other hand, when we switch on the television, choose a programme, cook a meal, go for a walk, there is a clear choice involved.

When deciding how far your son or daughter is already making decisions and when considering ways in which you could encourage him or her to take a more active part in making them, the following eight points may be useful. They describe eight different levels of involvement of the handicapped person in decision-making.

1) An event occurs which is not the result of decision-making.

2) An event occurs which results from the decision of someone outside the family (for example, the dentist sends a reminder for a dental check-up).

3) A decision is taken by the parent. The handicapped person is neither involved nor informed.

4) The handicapped person is informed of the decision which has been taken.

5) The handicapped person is asked how he or she feels about the decision, but the decision is not affected.

6) The decision is made jointly by the parent and handicapped person.

7) The handicapped person makes a decision for him/herself.

8) The handicapped person makes a decision which others, in the family or outside, will act upon.

We suggest that you use this as a reference list in order to discover whether it would be possible to involve your son or daughter at an earlier stage than at present in some of the decisions which affect him or her.

Ask yourself how many day-to-day decisions you make on his or her behalf, and whether these are necessary? Stop yourself when you find yourself making such a decision, and see how far you can involve your youngster.

Choosing the goal(s) to work towards
Decide jointly upon a limited objective. Do not attempt to tackle the most difficult problem first – you need to practise first with goals which are attainable in a fairly short time. Select something which is important to your son or daughter and in which you feel some progress can be made. Your own confidence in devising the teaching plan and recording progress, to be described in Chapters 6 and 7, will increase as you experience success.

We suggest that you read through your scale, and reflect on your long knowledge of your son or daughter, before writing a thumb-nail sketch of him or her. In this you should briefly describe the kind of person he or she is, stressing strengths and assets. In a separate space write down needs – the areas in which progress is desirable. State these needs in positive terms. For example, do not say 'he must stop making so much noise when eating', say instead 'he must learn to eat more quietly'. In Chapter 6, when describing how to design a teaching plan, we ask you to utilise as many as possible of your youngster's existing abilities when developing a new coping skill.

From the scale, and your description of the areas where further skills are needed, specific objectives can now be selected. An objective should be written down, and should say quite simply and clearly what your son or daughter will be doing when training has been completed. This may seem straightforward, but in our experience it can cause considerable difficulty, both to parents and to staff. We all need to practise being more precise, expressing ourselves in simple terms without ambiguity. Let us consider a few objectives, written in a vague way on the one hand and more precisely on the other:

Vague, Imprecise objectives	*Clear, Precise objectives*
Improves in personal hygiene	Washes hands before every meal
Uses money	Shops for items on grocery list and checks the change
Expresses himself better	Speaks more slowly
Cares for her appearance	Brushes her hair
Tells the time	Uses wristwatch to decide when to set off in the morning (8.30 a.m.)
Is Friendlier	
Is suitably dressed	
Uses the telephone	You try
Makes good use of leisure time	
Is tidier at home	

You can see that the examples listed in the left-hand column are vague and imprecise. They could be interpreted in a number of ways. In the right-hand column the objectives are both more precise and more limited. 'Cares for her appearance', for example, whilst stated in positive terms, is too vague to become a teaching objective. Whereas 'Brushes her hair', though only one way in which she may care for her appearance, can be made the specific target of a teaching programme. As you can see, we have completed five of the ten items, leaving it to you to think out precise objectives for the other five.

It is possible that you may choose an objective which is concerned with the *frequency* with which a particular ability is used. For example, your son or daughter may be able to tell the time, but may not make sufficient use of this. He or she may prefer to be awakened by you in the morning instead of being more independent. A suitable objective might be 'uses alarm clock to awaken at the appropriate time in the morning'.

In cases where the objective you select concerns the *frequency* with which an ability is used, you may find the list of frequencies presented in Chapter 1 useful. We set these frequencies out for you again below. Having written down the behaviour concerned, place the number in the box which describes the frequency with which the behaviour takes place at present. Next, after a discussion with your son or daughter, place the appropriate number in the box under the heading 'this is how often we would like it to happen'. In effect, you have now stated a precise objective. In Chapters 6 and 7 we show you how to modify the frequency of such behaviour, and how to record this.

Item	Frequency	This is how often it happens	This is how often we would like it to happen
1. (Insert the behaviour selected)	1. Never 2. Few times a year 3. Once a month 4. Few times a month 5. Once a week 6. Few times a week 7. Once a day 8. More than once a day	☐	☐

Taking Account of the Level of Independence when Choosing Objectives for Training

In the following figure, we bring together the various abilities listed in the assessment chart. Our intention is to indicate the way in which an individual's ability to cope independently in the community may be described as corresponding to a particular *level* of independence. The figure should be read from left to right, in the direction of increased independence. We feel that you will agree that a useful way of describing an individual's level of independence is in terms of the kind of living accommodation which would be suitable for him in the community. There are four levels shown in the figure.

In selecting the abilities to be listed together under a particular level of independence, we are suggesting that the individual should ideally be able to do each of these things, without help or supervision. This list is only a rough guide, as we know of no research which has established more precise criteria.

Read through the figure. You will see that it consists of 36 areas which are taken from the assessment chart. Refer back to the chart which you have completed, looking at each area in turn, and in the figure tick off those areas in which your son or daughter can do all five items.

Looking now at the pattern of ticks which you have placed in the figure, you should pay particular attention to levels 1 and 2. If your son or daughter is living at home with you, then we hope that all the areas listed under columns 1 and 2 will have been ticked. If not, then those areas which are not yet ticked should become high priorities. In this way, you will be consolidating the current level of coping.

The book, however, is concerned with extending the level of coping skills; so you should also be aiming to make inroads into skills required at level 3, living in a group home, or even higher.

When deciding on the allocation of the 36 areas to the 4 levels, as shown in the figure, the question we asked ourselves was: 'Could he or she get by, fairly comfortably, at that level if this area of skill is not present?' If our answer was 'no', then we entered the item in the column under that level, and also included it under all subsequent levels. The figure may

LEVEL 1. Maximum support available (e.g. hospital)	LEVEL 2. Moderate support available (e.g. home, or hostel)	LEVEL 3. Minimum support available (e.g. group home scheme)	No support, complete independence (e.g. flat)
	Leisure at home Number Colour recognition Table habits Setting and clearing table Social graces Grooming Dressing/Undressing	Sexual knowledge & behaviour Responsibility Leisure-group membership Friendships Conversation Personal knowledge Use of money Money Concept of time Telling the time Use of number Reading Shopping Public transport Community knowledge Tidying the room Making the bed Washing up Food and drink preparation Care of clothing Selection of clothing	Sexual knowledge & behaviour Responsibility Leisure-group membership Friendships Conversation Personal knowledge Use of money Money Concept of time Telling the time Use of number Reading Shopping Public transport Community knowledge Tidying the room Making the bed Washing up Food and drink preparation Care of clothing Selection of clothing
		Leisure at home Number Colour recognition Table habits Setting and clearing table Social graces Grooming Dressing/Undressing	Eating out Writing Telephone First aid and health Leisure at home Number Colour recognition Table habits Setting and clearing table Social graces Grooming Dressing/Undressing
Communication Hygiene Toilet	Communication Hygiene Toilet	Communication Hygiene Toilet	Communication Hygiene Toilet

Figure 5.

therefore be seen as a step-wise progress towards more independent functioning, or a greater level of coping.

In selecting your teaching objectives, you may find that the figure provides a useful overview of the degree of independence attained. You might wish, for example, to consolidate the abilities listed at a particular level, building upon strengths, before focusing on the next level. You will recall that in the scale we presented 36 areas, each of which consisted of five items, arranged in increasing order of difficulty. If, within any of these areas, you have been able to tick off three or four items, then consolidation would consist of attempting to teach your son or daughter the remaining one or two items within the area. For example, under 'Use of Telephone' your son or daughter may be able to answer a telephone, carry on a simple conversation, and even ring up individuals when the number is written down. He or she may not be able to use a call box, or a telephone directory. In this case, you could develop a teaching plan concerned with telephoning from a call box.

5 Examining resources available for teaching

Once you have completed your assessment chart, and made an initial selection of goals, you should begin thinking about the resources you will need to begin to teach. As you will see in the next chapter, on devising a teaching plan, you will be drawing up a list of the articles, materials, places and people you will need when the plan is put into action. In this chapter, we want to do some groundwork, explaining more fully what we mean by 'resources', and thereby helping you to recognise the opportunities which already exist within your home and neighbourhood.

By 'resources', in this context, we mean anything, anywhere, and anyone, able to be of service when helping your son or daughter to develop and cope more effectively. It is now accepted that an effective use of resources is the hallmark of a good teacher. Almost all schools have a resources cupboard or room; colleges of education and teachers' centres usually have well equipped 'resource centres'.

For almost all of the training exercises which we describe in Chapters 8, 9 and 10, you will find that no special materials or equipment need be purchased. As far as possible we have tried to suggest ways in which you might make good use of everyday things and situations. Some of you, however, may already have decided that more opportunities need to be created for your son or daughter to try out various activities. We have also considered in some detail the ways in which he or she may become more involved in decision-making and the choosing of objectives to work towards.

Teaching Resources in the Home

Take a look around your home, including the garden, or yard, if you have one. Have you ever thought of this as a learning area? Look around each room, or corridor. Have you ever stopped to notice all the possessions you have acquired? Where does the family spend most time – does this differ between members of the family? Do individuals have their own place for personal belongings? Which items, or parts of the home, tend to be shared by all? What about the atmosphere of the home, is it cheerful, bright, noisy?

Consider the household routine, how does this differ at weekends? How much of the routine revolves round specific times? Is time visible – do you have a grandfather clock, a wall clock, a clock on your kitchen cooker, for example? Do they all show the same time?

Is there a sense of order in terms of objects and articles within the house – do members of the household know where various things are stored? Do tools, crockery, cleaning materials, all have their own place? Are the shelves, cupboards or drawers ever labelled? In addition to helping with basic reading skills, labels can help to develop abstract concepts, categories into which things are grouped.

You could carry out an inventory of the various gadgets and appliances within the home. How many kinds of on-off switch are there? How many dials are to be found? Are there certain appliances which are rarely turned off (for example, the freezer, central heating boiler power switch)? Do some appliances carry a warning light when switched on (for example, immersion heaters, some types of electric kettle, electric fires)? What opportunities are there in the home for developing the use of number – commodities which need counting, weighing, or measuring in various ways? Sometimes numbers are used simply as labels – for examples, numbers on the television channel selector switches. Numbers on dials can stand for other things, for example, speed (record player turntable setting), temperature (wall thermometer), or size (the numbers on clothing labels, inside shoes, hats, gloves, and so on).

What opportunities exist for individual expression, for the development of a self-concept in the home? Are there mirrors, including a full length mirror, available? Do you have a family album showing individuals at different stages of development? Do you own a home movie outfit, or a slide projector, which can bring together experiences which have straddled the years? Does your son or daughter keep a diary containing essential biographical information, including: name, date of birth, height, colour of eyes, colour of hair, national health service number, and so on? Is there scope for displaying art work, models, swimming certificates, theatre programmes, or beer mats?

In connection with the development of basic reading skills, we have already mentioned the possibility of labelling cupboards, drawers, and so on. We should also consider the value of labels on jars, favourite brands of cereal, tinned food, and so on. Some homes have picture recipe cards, also calendars which show the fruit and vegetables available at different seasons. The Health Education Council have a series of educational posters which are useful and suitable for various parts of the house. Finally, check that labels such as 'Danger' and 'Poison' are clearly displayed where necessary in the household.

In reviewing the resources available within the home, you should not forget to include yourself! You, and members of the family, including relatives and friends who pop in from time to time, are the essential human resources available to help your youngster to develop into a more complete person. Your positive attitude and your cheerful optimism will go a long way to helping him or her to develop self-confidence.

Of course, there will be times when difficulties will loom large and you may feel tired and occasionally depressed. This is understandable, but it is exactly why it is important to try to develop a network of support among those around you. We discuss this more fully in Chapter 12.

Resources in the Neighbourhood

We suggest that you should explore these fully. Set out on a journey from home. Turn either to left or right and make a note of the presence or absence of various amenities within walking distance. Look also at road signs, street markings, the signs over various types of shops, the location of pedestrian crossings, post boxes, telephone kiosks. In order to help you, we have prepared the following list. We suggest that you tick off items from the list, adding others which occur to you.

Amenities In My Neighbourhood

Bank	Road/Street	Centre	Traffic signs
Post office	names	Special	Theatre
Town hall	Museum	school	Public house
Factories	Art gallery	Further	Swimming
Shops (local)	Airport	Education	baths
Shopping	Library	College	Post box
precinct	Cinema	Police station	Telephone
Department	Social club	Fire station	kiosk
stores	Sports centre	Dentist	Zebra
Public	Park	Doctor	crossing
toilets	Zoo	Optician	Pelican
Barber/	Job Centre	Information	crossing
Hairdresser	Adult	centre	Traffic
	Training	Supermarket	lights

Why not, in conjunction with an A-Z of your area, make a large scale chart of your immediate neighbourhood? Mark your house clearly upon the chart, together with the location of various amenities ticked on your list. We later suggest ways in which you might use this chart to create specific exercises for your son or daughter to carry out in the community. You may be interested to know that this is a standard approach adopted by some of the Diploma courses responsible for training teacher-instructors of mentally handicapped adults. Students on such courses make a similar chart when assigned to a Centre for teaching purposes.

Once again, as in the home, consider the ways in which the people, objects and places in the neighbourhood might serve as resources when teaching your son or daughter. Note the various routes which may be taken from home to such amenities as the supermarket, the Post Office, the Bank, Public Library, and so on. How important are signs – not just traffic signs, but signs for pedestrians, signs over shop windows, road and street names, advertisements and display posters? Note that some of these signs are permanent, others change frequently.

In how many places can numbers be seen, and how many different purposes do they serve? Note the prices shown on the window displays, contrast them to those shown over petrol pumps – what does 75.9p per gallon mean? Are you comfortable with volume when measured in litres rather than gallons, or with weights when measured in kilos, not pounds?

We soon begin to realise that there are many things in the community which, whilst possibly useful as teaching resources, can also prove confusing and difficult to understand. Indeed, walking around the neighbourhood specifically in order to pinpoint teaching resources in this way, can show us that many things in the past have gone unobserved. How does a police constable's uniform differ from that of a postman, or a fireman, for example? Would your son or daughter recognise the difference, or know what form of help or advice to get from each of these?

How well do you know the local shopkeepers? Would they be prepared to cooperate in your attempts to teach your son or daughter to carry out simple community expeditions, shopping with the use of a list, sometimes being required to check their own change? Would they cooperate to develop better communication, by reporting on the way in which your son or daughter delivered a simple or complex message?

Pay particular attention to leisure facilities, local cinemas, parks, theatres, discos and pubs, the swimming baths and possibly the sports centre. Are there any restrictions, or special difficulties, which your son or daughter has experienced in using them? Are entrances and exits clearly marked, pay-desks, enquiry areas, ladies' and gents' toilets? What signs need to be read which indicate the rules applying in the establishment – 'No Smoking' signs, 'No Dogs Allowed', 'Toilets', and so on. We hope you will develop and adapt some of the suggestions made here when devising teaching plans to be described in the next chapter. You will find that the first step in each teaching plan, after formulating your objective clearly, is to draw up a list of resources.

6   Techniques of teaching

You will recall that in Chapter 2 we emphasised the importance which *learning* plays in the development of human behaviour. Unlike many insects, birds, and animals, little of our behaviour is instinctive. Indeed, it is because man is so efficient at learning, at modifying his behaviour as a result of experience, that he has been able to dominate his environment. But learning does not take place in a vacuum – what a man learns is determined by his environment. For example, children in France learn to speak French.

We now understand much better the general rules which define what we learn. Earlier, we examined the stages involved in learning and considered the kinds of things that might go wrong. In this chapter we are going to describe the basic techniques of 'reward training'. These techniques have been found to be highly successful with individuals who experience learning difficulty. There is nothing essentially new in these techniques, good teachers have been using them for years. They do, however, combine certain principles in a systematic way, taking account of our improved knowledge of the learning process. Because the techniques are logical and straightforward, they can be understood and applied by people with little previous knowledge of educational theory or practice.

There are three essential parts to the learning situation – Cues or signals, behaviour, and consequences. These are related as shown in the following diagram:

We are concerned with the 'behaviour'. From the diagram we see that the 'cues' are events which precede the behaviour, and the 'consequences' are those things which result from the behaviour. Let us consider an example. When driving along, spots of rain appear on the windscreen. We switch on the windscreen wipers with the result that we once again see clearly. Note that it is the *consequences* which are of particular importance if we are concerned to change, or maintain behaviour. If the consequences are pleasant then the behaviour is rewarded, and there is an increased likelihood of its being repeated on a future occasion. If unpleasant, then the behaviour is not likely to be repeated so readily. If the windscreen wipers had been worn, for example, they might simply have smeared water and oil on the windscreen resulting in a blurry and reduced visibility.

We want you to concentrate on the results, or consequences, of behaviour, for this provides the key to modifying or improving it in most cases. This means that when you are acting as a teacher of your own son or daughter you should apply these principles, and become skilled in making use of those rewards which are most effective in their particular case. Each of us is different in the type, and amount, of reward needed to modify our behaviour.

Because we know that mentally handicapped individuals have more difficulty in learning simply from experience, we want you to structure experiences for them. In effect, you should become a 'manager' of the learning situation. This means that you should take the responsibility to ensure that the necessary cues are present (for example, by providing a demonstration), that the necessary behaviour can occur (for example, by breaking it down into small enough stages) and that a suitable reward is provided (for example, by saying 'Well done'). If your teaching does not produce the intended change in behaviour, then you should change your teaching strategy. This will become clearer when we go on to describe this teaching strategy and illustrate it with a number of examples.

In Chapter 4, we showed you how to select goals or objectives to work upon. On the basis of your completed assessment chart, you were encouraged to practise drawing up lists of your son's or daughter's individual 'strengths' and 'needs'. We then stressed the importance of involving him or her in this choice of goals to work towards. We have now reached the stage where we want you to develop teaching plans, based upon the principles of 'reward training'. In doing so, you will be attempting to make the most effective use of your son's or daughter's existing strengths.

Essentially, your close knowledge of the individual will help you in two ways. First, you will be able to choose, as your starting point, an area of ability in which some progress has already been made. You will be building upon previous success. Second, you will be in a good position to choose the most effective 'rewards', taking account of the interests which your son or daughter has expressed.

It is important to point out that the principles of reward training can be used for two different purposes. Sometimes we want to use them for developing new skills, for training behaviour which at present does not exist. Sometimes we are more concerned with *existing* behaviour – we may either wish to increase the behaviour, change it in some way, or attempt to eliminate it altogether. The term 'behaviour modification' is frequently used when reward training techniques are used to change existing behaviour. There are also other names in use, but throughout this book we will continue to use the term 'reward training'.

This book is concerned with developing coping skills, so we will first describe the use of reward training in helping your son or daughter to acquire new skills, in those areas of your assessment chart where you have found these to be lacking. We know, however, that many parents are anxious about what to do in the case of 'behaviour problems'. We are devoting a special section of this chapter to such problems, and will describe some special techniques which may be applied to reduce or eliminate unacceptable, anti-social, or injurious behaviour.

Developing New Abilities

The first necessity, as was seen in Chapter 4, is to be precise when defining the behaviour which you wish to develop. For example, parents sometimes say 'We'd like him to be more sociable'. But this could mean a number of things, it could mean making more friends, smiling more often, initiating conversation, joining a club, and so on. It can be seen that all of these, taken together, are aspects of 'being more sociable'. The important point, however, is that they can be seen as tangible, obtainable objectives, whereas 'being more sociable' is rather vague and immeasurable.

Once you have defined a clear objective, a new skill to be trained, you will need to analyse the task into its successive stages. This is rather like drawing up instructions for assembling a model kit, or writing a recipe for a new dish.

Analysing the Task

Let us consider an example of a task analysis – making a pot of tea for two, and serving it.

Objective: Makes a pot of tea for two and serves it.

Resources needed: Teapot, two cups, two saucers, four teaspoons, kettle, (electric or otherwise), stove (if kettle is not electric), tea or teabags, sugar, milk, cold water supply, milk jug, sugar bowl, serving tray.

Steps:
1. Remove the lid, or spout, from the kettle
2. Taking the kettle with the left hand (if you are right-handed), carry it over to the cold water tap and place beneath it

3. Turn on tap with right hand.
4. Turn off tap when kettle is half full
5. Carry kettle over to stove, or worktop
6. Replace spout, or lid, on kettle.
7. Plug in kettle (if electric) and switch on;

or

Light the gas ring, or turn on the electric ring, over which the kettle has been placed

8. Place teapot on the worktop
9. Take the lid off the teapot
10. Check that it is empty and ready to use
11. Take cups and saucers to the worktop
12. Place each cup upright on its own saucer
13. Place a teaspoon on each saucer beside the cup
14. Pour the milk into the milk jug, half filling it
15. Pour sugar into the sugar bowl, half filling it
16. Place one teaspoon in the sugar, handle uppermost.
17. Place cups and saucers, milk bowl and sugar bowl on the serving tray
18. When the kettle boils (whistles, produces large quantities of steam, or switches off automatically), remove it from heat (remove from the stove or switch off)
19. Pour a little boiling water into the teapot
20. Swish this around to heat the pot
21. Pour this water down the sink
22. Place three teaspoonsful of tea, or two tea bags, in the teapot
23. Carefully pour boiling water into the teapot until half full
24. Stir the contents of the teapot carefully two or three times
25. Replace the teapot lid
26. Carefully carry the teapot and place it on the serving tray
27. Carefully carry the serving tray across to the serving area, for example the sitting room

28. Place the serving tray on a convenient table, or ledge
29. Enquire whether the other person takes milk and sugar
30. Pour milk into each cup (as necessary), just filling the bottom
31. Holding the handle of the teapot in the right hand, place the first finger of the left hand upon the lid, holding it steady
32. Lift the teapot and pour tea into each cup in turn
33. Stop pouring when the tea is near the top of the cup
34. Replace the teapot upon the tray
35. Carefully lift one cup and saucer and pass it to the other person
36. Pick up the sugar bowl and hold it near to them (where sugar is required)
37. Wait until they have taken sugar, and replaced the spoon in the sugar bowl
38. Return sugar bowl to the tray
39. Proceed to put sugar (if required) in your own tea
40. Replace spoon in the sugar
41. Use the spoon in your own saucer for stirring your tea
42. Return spoon to saucer
43. Pick up teacup in your preferred hand and drink.

As you can see, there are 43 steps involved in this analysis. Indeed, some of the steps – for example, lighting the stove, or selecting the correct electric ring to switch on, or choosing the correct number of teaspoonsful of tea – could be broken down even further.

Let us look at another example, changing a fuse in an electric plug. This is the kind of practice exercise which is used to train industrial analysts in the principles of job analysis. In this example, we will describe what each hand will be doing at each stage in the operation. On our 'analysis sheet', the movements made by the left hand are written on the left hand side of the central line, whilst those made by the right hand are written on the right hand side of the line (assuming you are right-handed).

Resources needed: Three-pin plug, new fuse (of the correct ampage), screwdriver, worktop.

Steps:

Left hand	Right hand
1. Reach for plug	Reach for screwdriver
2. Move plug towards screwdriver	Place screwdriver in slot in screw in back of plug
3. Grip plug tight	Begin to unscrew
4. Fingers close around screw	Continue unscrewing (about 6 turns)
5. Grip screw	Place screwdriver on bench
6. Release screw, still holding plug	Take screw
7.	Place screw on bench
8. Assist	Take hold of cover of plug
9. Assist	Remove cover
10.	Place cover on bench
11.	Pick up screwdriver
12.	Insert tip under old fuse
13. Assist	Prise fuse out from one end of its holder
14.	Take fuse with fingers
15.	Place fuse on bench
16.	Pick up new fuse
17.	Place it in one end of holder
18. Assist	Press into holder
19. Assist	Press other end of fuse until it clicks into holder
20.	Pick up cover
21. Move plug towards cover	Place cover in position

Left hand	Right hand
22.	Press shut
23.	Pick up screw from bench
24. Assist by positioning plug	Place screw in hole in cover
25.	Start thread by turning fingers
26.	Pick up screwdriver
27. Fingers close around screw, supporting it	Locate in slot in screw
28.	Screw up tight (about 6 turns)
29. Place plug on bench	Place screwdriver on bench

In the above example you can see that 29 steps were involved. In fact, in many parts of the analysis, both hands were working together, appearing on the same line. This had the effect of reducing the total number of steps involved. In most examples of task analysis, however, these steps are simply written down as a continuous list, as in our first example.

It is now your turn to try. First, equip yourself with a few sheets of paper and a pencil. Imagine that you are about to cook poached egg on toast for one person. Write out the headings as shown below:

Objective:

Resources needed:

Steps: 1.
      2.
      3.
      etc.

Once you have made these headings on your paper, you should first write your objective in clear positive terms, such as: 'Makes poached egg on toast for one person'. Secondly, you should list the resources required. Next, write out the steps that you would follow. Write each step on a new line and number it. Do not make these steps too big or too small, but imagine that your analysis is actually to be followed by another person – so don't miss out anything important! When you have finished, turn to the end of this chapter where you can compare your analysis with one we made. How many steps did *you* take? How did your analysis compare with ours?

We suggest that Mum and Dad should set each other a task to analyse, and then take it in turns to follow as literally as possible the instructions which the other has written down. This can be both fun, and very illuminating! You could choose items from the assessment chart, or any other activity in the daily routine. Start with a task which does not have too many steps, before progressing to more complex tasks. You could, for example, choose from the following list of suggestions:

Making a telephone call; changing the bed sheets and pillowcases and making the bed; cleaning your teeth; cleaning and polishing shoes; making a journey by bus; shaving; tying a knot in a necktie (a Windsor knot is a greater challenge); laying places at the table in preparation for a meal for four persons; washing hair.

Much of of our daily routine behaviour is complex. It consists of long chains of activities. It has been found that if there are a large number of steps involved in completing a particular task, sometimes it is easier for the learner if you teach the last step first. In other words, some lengthy behaviours might be better learnt 'backwards'. Below, we list the basic steps involved in tying a simple knot in a necktie.

1. Lift collar
2. Fasten collar button

D

3. Place tie around neck – with wide end in right hand, narrow end in left hand

4. Pull tie down on right side so that twice as much tie is on right, compared with left, side

5. Cross right hand over left

6. Release and move hand back towards right

7. Move right hand under tie by left hand and grip wide end

8. Pull this under, towards the right

9. Regrasp and place right (wide) piece over the left

10. Release and move hand back towards right

11. Move right hand under tie held by left hand, and grip wide end once again

12. Pull this downwards

13. Thread it up through the inside of the loop, next to the shirt, gripping the knot gently with fingers of right hand

14. Release grip on narrow end with left hand

15. Bring left hand up to the top

16. Continue pulling the wide end through the loop with left hand

17. Use thumb of right hand to slacken the front of the knot

18. Push wide end of tie through the front of the knot, using the first two fingers of the left hand

19. Move the left hand to replace the right hand in gripping the front of the knot

20. Lower the right hand to grip the wide end below the knot

21. Finish pulling it through

22. Left hand now grips the front (wide) end and right hand grips the back piece

23. Both hands pull down, tightening the knot

24. Right hand continues to grasp narrow (back) piece whilst left thumb and forefinger encircle base of the knot

25. Right hand pulls down whilst left hand pushes the knot gently up
26. Stop when knot reaches collar height
27. Left hand drops and grasps wide (front) end once again and jerks (twice) the knot tight
28. Left hand moves knot left, or right, to be central, opposite collar button
29. Both hands are raised to grip back edge of upturned collar
30. Pull collar down, sliding fingers round to front when doing so
31. Make final central adjustment, if necessary.

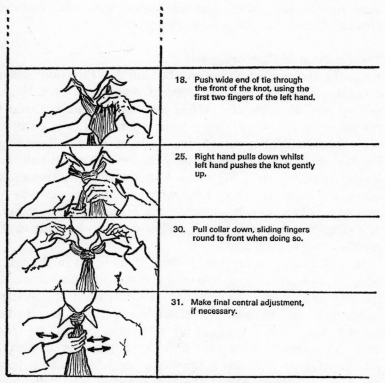

18. Push wide end of tie through the front of the knot, using the first two fingers of the left hand.

25. Right hand pulls down whilst left hand pushes the knot gently up.

30. Pull collar down, sliding fingers round to front when doing so.

31. Make final central adjustment, if necessary.

Figure 6. Final stages in an example of task analysis.

As you can see, even this simple knot involved 31 stages. It is a good example of the type of task which could be taught backwards. One advantage of this system is that the learner always finishes up by completing the task. If he should start from the beginning, in the more usual way, he might get stuck at one or two points and forget what the final objective looks like. We shall illustrate some of these final stages for you, starting with the final step in the task – that is the first step for a learner who is being taught the task 'backwards'.

Once a lengthy task has been broken down into steps, it is a question of individual judgement, and confidence, whether teaching should be forwards, or backwards. There are no fixed rules – you should feel free to use whichever method appears most suitable in a particular case.

The Function of Cues or Signals

From the above examples, it can be seen that behaviour often consists of long 'chains' of different operations, or actions, carried out in sequence. When we observe an individual carrying out a task involving many operations, we see only his behaviour. In terms of our diagram of the 'Learning Process' in Chapter 2, we see only the actions which link the learner with the task. We know however that the learner is doing a number of other things which we cannot see – he is selecting which signals entering his senses are important, attending to them, remembering what needs to be done next, deciding how to do it and so on.

How does the learner know where he is up to in the task, what to do next? This is where it becomes useful to think of the task as a chain of behaviour. The completion of one step in the task acts as a cue, or signal, for the next step to be carried out. In our example of making a pot of tea, for example, completion of step 5 (carry kettle over to stove) provides the cue for step 6 (replacing the lid), which in turn provides the cue for step 7 (lighting the gas). The individual learns to link each step to the previous one, like adding links to a chain. Of course, the more experience he has in carrying out the complete task, the stronger the links become, and the more able he is able to see the task as a whole. At this stage, by anticipating several steps in advance, he may be able to discover short cuts, or find that some parts of the task may be carried out in a different order.

Cues, or signals, are familiar features of everyday life. They are all around us, acting as triggers for our behaviour. We learn to respond appropriately to traffic lights, ringing telephones, door chimes, and so on. But perhaps the most important type of cue is the spoken word – greetings, commands and questions all require a response. So the language we use in teaching is clearly critical to our success. If the learner does not possess the necessary vocabulary, then we must either teach this vocabulary or, better still, use simpler words where possible. The correct words will be easier to apply once the task itself has been mastered.*

If the learner does not understand the meaning of the words we use to direct his actions, then they cannot act as cues, or triggers. For this reason, whenever you carry out a task analysis, we would like you to make a list of the vocabulary which the task requires. Choose simple words, where alternatives are possible. Then attempt to be consistent in the use of these words whilst teaching. For example, 'Put it on the top', pointing to the side of the kitchen sink, may be easier to follow than 'Put it on the drainer'.

Whilst language, carefully used, can be a valuable aid to teaching tasks, it is also true that learning certain tasks can help with the development of language. We observed earlier that much of what is going on in the learner's mind cannot be observed – we can only see the actions which result from it. Research has shown that it is useful, in the initial stages of

---

*A well known research worker in the USA, Marc Gold, has stressed the dangers of using too much, and too complex, language when teaching new skills. He uses the expression 'try another way' as a general way of indicating to the learner that he is not performing correctly.

learning, for the learner to recite aloud the actions which he is performing, as they occur. Because we think in words, this helps to strengthen the link between the various stages in the chain of behaviour which the task requires. Now, not only does the learner see the kettle placed on the worktop, he says 'Next I put it here – now I put on the lid'.

In addition to spoken language, we make use of other important cues when teaching. Gestures, such as pointing, or nodding, are used to mean 'Place it there', or 'Start now'. Deaf people have developed a whole language of signs to represent things and feelings, just as we use spoken words. So, just as we must be careful in choosing the vocabulary we use in teaching, so we should be aware of the way in which we use gestures. Once again, these signs or cues should be easy to understand, unambiguous, and used in a consistent way.

Remember, in our earlier example of the learner driver, how difficult it was to know what should be attended to. The learner gains confidence and makes progress precisely because the driving instructor adopts a consistent vocabulary, and method of demonstrating. He is there to point out, at each stage in the task, what the learner should be attending to.

You should now be much clearer about the role which cues play in teaching. They help to focus the learner's attention to the important feature of the task, even if there is a good deal of background noise and distraction. Sometimes the teacher will exaggerate the cue, for example by speaking louder, or nodding more vigorously. The purpose of it all, however, is that the learner should eventually be able to carry out the task alone. We must teach him to attend to the cues within the task itself, fading out our own gestures as soon as possible.

In Chapter 10, when describing the development of inter-personal skills, we will consider the use of more subtle cues. Changes in facial expression, for example a frown, or a raised eyebrow, serve as cues indicating our feelings. They provide a good example of an area of skill which mentally handicapped individuals often have difficulty in acquiring merely from experience. They cannot be neglected, however, because they greatly influence the effect we have on the behaviour of others.

The Role of Reward

We stated earlier that we wanted you to concentrate on the results, or consequences, of behaviour. When teaching an individual to carry out a new task, the value of using some form of reward is two-fold. First, it tells the learner that the action which he has just performed was correct, or acceptable. We say it gives him 'knowledge of results' – without it, he cannot learn. Second, because the reward is present, the learner will be more likely to want to repeat the action on a subsequent occasion.

Much of what is known about the effective use of rewards results from work in training animals and young children. But clearly, the nature of 'reward' must be adapted to suit the individual case. When dealing with adolescents and young adults, we cannot treat them like children, so the sweets, kisses or hand-clapping recommended in teaching children are less appropriate. We have already referred to the special significance of presenting the task as a challenge to which the individual might respond, so that success becomes itself the reward. The use of a smile, a wink, a handshake, a slap on the back, or a simple 'Well done', is frequently sufficient to reinforce the success, and encourage the youngster.

An essential element in the use of any kind of reward is *timing*. When rewards are used, they should always follow immediately the behaviour which we are trying to strengthen. In the initial stages of learning, reward may be necessary at frequent intervals in order to encourage the individual to continue through the various stages of the task. It is more adult, however, to allow silence itself to be a reward wherever possible. In other words, we can show by our close attention to what he or she is doing that we are interested and pleased with progress. You must use your own judgement here, but one successful research worker has shown that carrying out a demanding task provides its own intrinsic reward – we can often reserve our jubilant comment until after the individual has completed it.

If it should be necessary to use more basic rewards, such as sweets, or a drink, then it is important that these should always be accompanied by 'secondary rewards' – smiles, praise, and so on. The reason for this is that the use of such basic rewards is artificial, and clearly cannot always be provided whenever the individual is to perform the task. Sometimes, as in the case of an individual with a weight problem, basic rewards such as food and drink could be unhealthy.

We have stressed the importance of involving your son or daughter as fully as possible at every stage. He or she has an important part to play not only in selecting the goal, but also in determining the kind of reward to use. Although the achievement of completing a task will in itself be a reward, this could be supplemented by a special treat. Ask your son or daughter what you should all do together when this new skill has been learnt. You could plan a trip to the cinema, go out for a meal, or he or she could invite a special friend round for a meal. If possible, try to combine this treat with an opportunity to use the new skill concerned. If a friend is invited round, for example, then this would be an excellent opportunity to apply that new skill of making a pot of tea!

One effective way of rewarding your son or daughter, in a way that is both adult and easy to interpret, is by means of a 'personal record card'. This is intended to fit easily into an inside pocket or handbag, and should be filled in by the parent but kept for personal reference by the mentally handicapped individual. It should show him or her how well goals are being met and may form a basis for a weekly 'treat'. We describe how to make and use such a card, together with other recording systems, in Chapter 7.

Finally, we should say something about the use of 'negative rewards'. An example of a 'negative reward' would be shaking the head when a mistake is made: just as, when the individual was a child, you might have administered a smack as a quick, clear, indication that the previous behaviour should not be repeated. But from the learner's point of view, a positive reward (a nod) and a negative one (shake of the head) serve the same purpose, in that they both inform him whether the action was correct or not. The main point to make here is that we want you to become as *positive* as possible in your approach to teaching. We want to ensure that your son or daughter continues to want to learn the task. Although we all learn from our mistakes, it is much more pleasant to be praised for our correct performance than to be criticised when we make a mistake. So part of our aim should be to ensure success. By breaking down any task into small enough steps, and providing a clear demonstration at each stage, you can minimise the number of possible mistakes. And remember that almost all behaviour is learned – if we allow the individual to develop bad habits, or incorrect methods of performing a task, then these have to be *unlearned*.

Preparing the Teaching Plan
Having selected a clear goal or objective, you should write out clearly what your son or daughter will be able to do when training is complete. You should make a work book (a spring clip file would be suitable) and write down each new goal on a separate sheet in the book. On a second sheet you should list the resources which you are going to need during the task – you may refer back to Chapter 5 when doing so.

D*

Not only may various materials, or objects, be required, you should also decide *who* is going to be involved in the teaching, and where it is to take place. On the lower half of this sheet you should make a list of all the words relevant to the task that the learner should know in spoken and written form.

On a third sheet you should write out your step-by-step analysis of the task itself. We suggest that you do this on the left-hand side of the sheet, leaving space on the right-hand side to write down the instructions, gestures and rewards you plan to use at each stage. In doing so, think carefully about the interests and aspirations which your son or daughter has expressed during your discussions about selecting this goal. In preparing your teaching plan, you should attempt to combine as many as possible of these interests.

Your plan should describe clearly not only how you are going to teach the particular skill, but how you are going subsequently to provide opportunities for the skill to be tried out. If you are teaching how to use the telephone, for example, then you should build in good reasons for making regular use of a telephone. If you are teaching your son or daughter to cook a simple meal, plan an evening when friends come round and the skill can be put to use.

It remains for you to indicate, in your plan, the time-scale within which it will operate. Look back at your step-by-step analysis, and place a date beside the first step. This is the date upon which you intend to commence training. Using your judgement, attach dates to various stages in the task. These are the dates by which you hope your son or daughter will be able to carry out these stages in the task, without help or prompting. Of course, the time between dates will depend upon the complexity of the task, and the number of stages involved. We strongly recommend, however, that they should be not more than one week apart.

You yourself need to be rewarded by seeing progress, and if such progress is not being achieved within this period of time, then you will need to change your strategy. Either the steps in the task are too large, or the rewards are not sufficiently effective. In the next chapter we discuss more fully the need for recording, and show how you should do this. The kinds of records suggested are not time consuming, or difficult to complete. You will find them invaluable as a means of checking upon the progress that is being made.

We are now going to give you an example of a teaching plan, illustrating points which we have just made. We will then conclude this section by presenting a summary of teaching hints which result from research and practice. This summary will serve to complement the basic teaching principles which we have just described.

An Example of a Teaching Plan

Objective:	Setting a place at table – he will be able to name and select the items required, and arrange them on the table in the correct position.
Resources needed:	Materials: large sheet of paper (18″ x 12″), pencil, knife, fork, soup spoon, dessert spoon, side plate, dinner plate, soup plate, glass, napkin, place mat.
Language needed:	Table, place, setting, fork, knife, spoon, soup, dessert plate, glass, napkin, mat, left, right, middle, side.

Task analysis	Teaching method	Date
He will:	First, prepare a 'shadow-	
Step 1 Put place mat on rectangle drawn on white sheet	board', showing outline of place setting, all items in correct position.	
Step 2 Put dinner plate on place mat	Carry out detailed task-analysis (as in left-hand	
Step 3 Fold napkin and place on left of dinner plate	column). Check that your son or daughter wants to learn	2 January
Step 4 Place fork on napkin	the task. Say: 'Here are the things we will need, and	

Task analysis	Teaching method	Date
Step 5 Place knife on right of dinner plate	this (pointing to the drawn outline) shows where the things will go. You watch me, and then you can try.' Place each item on the position marked, naming it as you do so.	
Step 6 Place side plate on small circle marked		
Step 7 Place glass where shown on paper		
Step 8 Place dessert spoon above plate handle to the right	Remove them all, and then allow your son or daughter to try. Hand each item in turn, pointing to its position.	
Step 9 Place soup spoon next to knife	Remove all items and repeat, this time naming items as you hand them to him or her.	
Step 10 Pointing to main objects		
Step 11 Naming the objects	Say: 'Good, well done', 'Make it look like this', and so on.	
Step 12 Repeating this		
Step 13 Doing it without the sheet	Then try it with the drawn outline removed, once again naming the items as you demonstrate.	16 January
Step 14 Collecting the objects and doing it without the sheet	Finally, try the task without assembling the items, tell son or daughter to go to the drawers, etc., to get what is required, naming the items once assembled, if possible.	23 January
Step 15 Practice: set own place for evening meal	Note: if language is a problem, still teach the task in sequence, naming objects yourself – this frequent repetition of the correct names of items may help receptive language to develop.	
	Finally: Let task be tried on an evening when company are expected, praising the help which he or she can now give.	30 January

Your teaching plans need not be as detailed as this, though you may find a number of other examples where it would be useful to provide a diagram to explain to your son or daughter what is required in the task. We sometimes call this using a 'shadow board'. Your diagram could refer to a larger area, for example, the floor plan of their own room where you indicate by diagrams where various things should be stored and put away neatly after use: shoes in one corner, books, records and so on.

Now you practise making your own teaching plans – taking the time to write them out in the way shown. Use these main headings as they will remind you what you did, should you ever need to return to this task at a later date in order to revise the skill. Be sure to explain to your son or daughter what you are doing, and provide the opportunity for it to be put to good use in future.

Summary of Teaching Principles, plus Further Hints

The main teaching principles have now been illustrated – we will briefly recap on these, and then present further hints derived from research.

1. Insist that each operation be carried out correctly before proceeding to the next – remember that incorrect performance only results in habits which have to be unlearned.
2. Ensure success by presenting only a small step at a time.
3. Use simple language and clear gestures. Speak slowly and distinctly, and be consistent in your use of words.
4. Inform the learner whether his performance is correct or not. During the early stages of learning, correct behaviour should be rewarded immediately, by saying 'Good', or 'That's right'. As the learner progresses with the task, reward him by your silence and interest, only saying 'Well done' when the task is completed.

Further useful hints:

5. Space your teaching sessions out over time. Three sessions of 20 minutes each are likely to be more effective than one session of an hour.

6. Once the task has been mastered, ensure that it is practised several times more. It has been found that this 'over-learning' is a powerful way of ensuring that the task will not readily be forgotten.

7. Make full use of the different senses when teaching. Ensure that the learner not only sees, but also hears what is involved. Help him to feel the correct movements, for example, by standing behind him and 'moulding' his actions until he gets the feeling of the correct movements involved.

8. Provide opportunities for this new knowledge or skill to be transferred to a different setting. For example, if teaching your son or daughter to make a pot of tea, perhaps he or she could practise this in the home of a relative, using a different teapot, type of cooker, and so on.

9. In addition to motivating the individual by pointing out the challenge which has been overcome, discuss the advantages it has for greater independence. Show your enthusiasm and admiration for the progress made, emphasising the success which this represents.

10. Give the learner the opportunity to show others how it is done – a younger brother or sister, for example. The chance to act as a teacher is one which is greatly appreciated by many mentally handicapped people. Recent research has shown that they can be most effective teachers, and experiments in 'pyramid teaching' have proved very popular.

So far we have described the application of reward training principles to the development of new skills. In Chapters 8, 9 and 10 we outline a number of exercises around which you can design teaching plans to develop skills within the three principal areas of coping. As we promised earlier, however, we will now turn our attention to the application of reward training to cases of 'behaviour disorder'.

Problem Behaviour and How to Deal With It

If an individual is to be accepted by others, his behaviour must correspond to that which is expected of his age, sex, and the culture in which he lives. A major concern of many parents is the inappropriateness of certain aspects of their handicapped son's or daughter's behaviour. More than the lack of knowledge or skills, this often serves to draw attention to the individual and can produce difficulties or embarrassment for the immediate family. In a child such behaviour may have been more tolerated – people expect children to be 'naughty' occasionally. If such behaviours persist or develop during the adolescent or adult stage, society is less tolerant.

It is of course true that many of the behaviours, labelled 'immature', or 'problem', are also found among non-handicapped youngsters passing through the difficult adolescent stage. It is important to recognise this, and it should not be assumed that mentally handicapped individuals will have more behaviour problems, or more severe problems, than other individuals. We believe that in all cases such behaviour is learned, in the same way that good behaviours or skills relevant to coping, are also learned.

Examples of inappropriate behaviour include: threatening others; bossing others around; talking too loudly; talking excessively; smiling or giggling excessively, or at the wrong time; stubbornness; swearing; avoiding others; excessive reaction to criticism; failing to anticipate the consequences of actions; excessive, or inappropriate, physical contact; self-injurious behaviour, for example scratching or picking; unpleasant personal habits; violent loss of temper.

Not all behaviour needing to be eliminated, or modified,

should strictly speaking be regarded as 'problem behaviour'. It may simply be a little odd or unusual, likely to draw attention to the individual. Sometimes, this behaviour is fine – it is simply the time or place at which it occurs that is unfortunate. Laughter in the public library, or in church, is an example of this.

When applying the principles of reward training to the modification or elimination of behaviour problems, the basic assumption is that such undesirable behaviour has been learned. In the past, the consequences of the behaviour have served to 'reward' it, making it more likely to recur. In order to remove the behaviour problem, therefore, it is necessary to analyse the situation in which it occurs in order to discover the cues which trigger it, and the way in which the consequences serve to reward it.

Let us consider an example.

Case Number 1

Ralph is a mentally handicapped young man aged 19. He lives at home with his parents and a brother who is two years younger. Ralph likes watching television and is beginning to dominate the family viewing – becoming quite aggressive when anyone wishes to change channels whilst he is watching a favourite programme. He jumps up and swears and pushes the other person aside, turning back to the previous programme. Ralph's parents have tried to reason with him, explaining that he should be reasonable, and less selfish. This always proves fruitless and they end up by giving way for the sake of peace and quiet. They cannot afford to buy a second television set.

When considering this example, we should try to identify the three important elements involved, what behaviour needs to be modified, what is it that triggers this behaviour, and how is it being rewarded.

For a considerable time Ralph has succeeded, by

swearing and brute force, in obtaining his own way. Although his family would like him to have some say in what should be viewed, they find it hard to tolerate his aggressive outbursts. Unwittingly, however, by giving in on previous occasions, they have strengthened this negative behaviour. Ralph has learned that swearing and force are powerful ways of getting his own way. In fact, members of the family have come to accept that the only way of obtaining peace and quiet is to give way. Thus, the peace which follows can be seen to be rewarding their own behaviour.

How can Ralph's behaviour be improved? The important thing to do is to ensure that in future this behaviour is not rewarded. One way of achieving this would be to switch off the television set, or unplug it, whenever such an incident occurred. No doubt Ralph would object to this, but the family must agree to ignore him, not speaking to him or looking at him, until he is quiet. At this point, involve him in a discussion about choice of programmes. You might, for example, suggest that each member of the family, including Ralph, take a turn in choosing the programme. Better still, you could build this into a teaching plan concerned with improving Ralph's decision-making skills.

By reference to published programme details, you could make a wall chart. In this you could show the dates, times, and channels, of Ralph's favourite programmes. This would show that you do intend to take account of his interests, just as he must do for other members of the family. Into this chart, therefore, it might be possible also to include times which are reserved for his brother, for example, to view a particular programme.

In this example, two important points are illustrated. First, the consequences of Ralph's negative behaviour are changed, since the reward of watching television does not follow his swearing or aggressive behaviour. Second, this negative behaviour is replaced by positive behaviour – he is required to be quiet and reasonable before television viewing is resumed. Wherever possible the behaviour which is to be eliminated should be replaced by something positive, ideally by something which is incompatible with the problem behaviour. An important principle in this is to be consistent.

Let us consider another example.

Case Number 2

Janet is aged 22 and lives at home with her widowed mother. She is quite attractive and very affectionate – too much so in fact. Mother is beginning to worry at the ease with which she smiles at strangers. When a visitor calls to the house, she readily greets them with an embrace and sometimes a kiss. In most cases, strangers react to this with good humour, tinged with embarrassment. During their frequent conversations, mother has tried discussing this with Janet, but is afraid of damaging her warm personality.

In considering this example, and any others, we want you to answer the following questions in turn:

1. What is the behaviour which needs to be eliminated?
2. What cue, event, or situation, seems to trigger it off?
3. What appears to be rewarding or maintaining the behaviour?
4. How can this reward be removed?
5. What positive, incompatible, behaviour should take the place of the behaviour being eliminated?
6. How is the success of this approach going to be measured and recorded?

Our brief answer to the above questions would be as follows:

Answer 1: Smiling at, embracing, and kissing strangers.
Answer 2: The presence of a stranger, especially a visitor to her home.

Answer 3: The stranger's smile and good humoured response.

Answer 4: Mother needs some help here from a number of individuals not known to Janet who agree to help, either by visiting the house, or in some other setting. They should be briefed not to respond too readily when Janet smiles at them (this part of her behaviour we wish to modify, not eliminate entirely). If Janet should step forward to embrace them they should step back, saying 'No'.

Answer 5: Janet should be taught the appropriate greeting behaviour which should be used after a stranger has been introduced. She has a good command of language. Her previous embrace should be replaced by a handshake, but only if initiated by the person to whom she has been introduced. Following this correct behaviour, mother should smile at Janet, later remarking that she behaved perfectly.

Answer 6: Mother should keep a simple checklist, to be completed each day. Before commencing her attempt to modify Janet's behaviour, she could record, for each occasion concerned, whether Janet behaved appropriately in the presence of a stranger. She could use a tick, for example, to represent appropriate behaviour and a cross to represent inappropriate behaviour. She may wish, instead of a cross, to use the letters 'S', 'E', 'K', or 'H', to represent a smile, embrace, kiss, or handshake. During the period when mother, with some cooperation from others, is attempting to modify Janet's behaviour, some record should be maintained. The record must be able to show not only the reduction in Janet's inappropriate behaviour, but also the increase in the substituted appropriate behaviour. Scores for successive weeks could be worked out to enable a pattern to be seen more clearly. (For a more detailed description of how to record progress, see Chapter 7.)

It is now your turn to practise using these six questions to analyse a problem. Following the next example, we have written out the questions for you, with a space for you to respond. Having done so, you may wish to compare your responses to ours by turning to page 121.

Case Number 3

Gary, aged 16, is the youngest of a large family. He lives at home with his parents and one sister who is shortly to be married. He has recently begun attending the local Adult Training Centre, where he has shown an above average level of manual skill. As his sister's wedding is approaching, his parents are keen that he should play an active part in the day. They are concerned, however, about the unsightly blemishes on his face. Following a slight skin irritation, for the past few weeks Gary has been continually picking at his face. They have noticed that his picking is worse when they are discussing the wedding plans in his presence. Mother usually goes over and sits by him, restraining his hands, and telling him not to pick, as it spoils his looks. This usually works for a short time, but the frequency of picking is gradually increasing.

This is a more difficult example and provides you with a good test of whether or not you are beginning to grasp the basic principles of reward training, and how they might be applied to a range of difficult problems. Here are the questions for you to consider:

1. What is the behaviour which needs to be eliminated?

2. What cue, event, or situation, seems to trigger it off?

3. What appears to be rewarding or maintaining the behaviour?

4. How can this reward be removed?

5. What positive, incompatible, behaviour should take the place of the behaviour being eliminated?

6. How is the success of this approach going to be measured and recorded?

If your son or daughter has a particularly difficult problem, then you have no doubt already sought expert advice. You may have experienced difficulty in obtaining this, as the powerful techniques of behaviour modification have only recently begun to be included in programmes of staff training. Because the techniques described are all based upon sound educational principles, we are optimistic about their wider application. Many staff recognise the challenge which problem behaviour offers as a test of their professional skills. Although in the past 'behaviour problems' have been a frequent reason for wishing not to accept an applicant into a training programme, we are convinced that this situation will improve.

Having read this chapter you should now feel more confident about embarking upon a programme of training which is relevant to your son's or daughter's needs. You have carried out a comprehensive assessment, considered the skills which need to be developed or put to better use, and you have taken your son's or daughter's wishes into account when deciding upon priorities and selecting the rewards. You have had some practice in developing a teaching plan with a realistic timescale, making the most of the resources available in your home and neighbourhood.

Now you need to know whether or not you are making progress. Not only you, but also your son or daughter needs to know this. In the next chapter we describe more fully the various methods of keeping records, including ways of doing so which involve your youngster and can be easily understood by all concerned.

Our solution to task set on page 96: Cooking poached egg on toast for one person

Objective: He/she cooks poached egg on toast for one person.

Resources needed: Materials needed: Two eggs, two slices of bread, egg-poacher, water supply, stove or cooking-ring, butter, plate, knife, timer (assuming no automatic toaster).

Language needed: Egg, bread, eggshell, butter, water, poaching pan (or 'poacher'), tap, stove, cooking ring, light switch, one, two, lid, time, timer, heat, slices, grill, toast, brown, plate, knife, off.

Steps:

1. Remove egg containers from poaching pan.
2. Take poaching pan to cold water tap.
3. Half fill with water.
4. Place on stove or cooking ring.
5. Light, or switch on the ring.
6. Set to medium heat.
7. Take two of the egg containers.
8. Use knife to place 'knob' of butter in each.
9. Replace them in poacher pan, in holding ring.
10. Place remaining egg container(s) (though empty) also in holding ring, so all spaces are full.
11. Take one egg and hold over poaching pan.
12. Tap middle of egg with blade of knife until cracked.
13. Carefully empty egg into one of the egg containers which contains knob of butter.
14. Place empty eggshell on worktop.
15. ⎫
16. ⎬ Repeat steps 11 to 14 with
17. ⎪ second egg.
18. ⎭
19. Place lid on poaching pan.

20. Note time, or set timer.
21. Light or switch on cooker grill.
22. Set to medium heat.
23. Place two slices of bread under grill.
24. Monitor cooking, watch toast and timer.
25. When timer shows 3 minutes have elapsed, *carefully* lift lid of poacher and check eggs.
26. If tops have turned white, are fairly firm, remove pan from heat.
27. When toast is brown on one side, turn over.
28. Turn off grill when this side is also brown.
29. Place toast on plate.
30. Use knife to spread butter on one side of each piece of toast.
31. Remove lid from poacher, carefully (it should have cooled down a little by now).
32. Lift out one egg container *carefully* (watch for steam).
33. Hold over the toast, slightly upside down.
34. Use knife to ease egg gently out and onto toast.
35. ⎫ Repeat steps 32 to 34 with
36. ⎬ other egg onto second piece of
37. ⎭ toast.
38. Turn off any remaining heat.
39. Place poaching pan and egg con-containers plus holding ring aside to be cleaned.

Poached egg on toast is now ready to eat!

Suggested Answers to the Questions Posed During Analysis of Case Number 3, Page 116

1. What is the behaviour which needs to be eliminated?
   Gary's picking at his face.

2. What cue, event, or situation, seems to trigger it off?
   We cannot be absolutely certain what is acting as the trigger for this behaviour. It appears that discussion of the wedding plans increases the likelihood of it recurring.

3. What appears to be rewarding or maintaining the behaviour?
   As the frequency of the behaviour is increasing, we suuggest that it is the attention which mother gives to him, sitting by him and telling him not to pick, which is rewarding the behaviour. Her physical contact in restraining his hands, together with remarks about his 'looks', suggests that he is obtaining some attention for the behaviour.

4. How can this reward be removed?
   There are a number of possibilities here. In addition to attempting to avoid the situation which seems to trigger the behaviour – talking about the wedding in his presence – Mother should avoid attending to Gary when he is picking. Of course, if the problem is quite severe, then it cannot be ignored. It may be necessary, for example, to make him wear gloves for a period.

5. What positive, incompatible, behaviour should take the place of the behaviour being eliminated?
   We know that Gary has shown considerable manual skill. By giving him something to do with his hands, keeping them busy, he cannot at the same time be picking his face. He could be encouraged to make a suitable wedding present, a small piece of furniture for example, in readiness for his sister's wedding. For using his hands constructively in this way he should be given a good deal of praise. This might also provide the key

to his involvement in the wedding plans. His possible apprehension may be lessened if he is looking forward to presenting the wedding gift, the nature of which could become a well kept secret between himself and his parents.

6. How is the success of this approach going to be measured and recorded?

On a small chart, taped on the inside of the kitchen cabinet, for example, Mother could enter the number of times Gary has been observed picking at his face during each day. This record can be completed very quickly, and daily totals can be compared over the period of a week. They should show the picking is beginning to diminish.

7 Recording progress

You have already had practise in writing down the stages involved in a task, and in planning your teaching programmes. Before this, in Chapters 3 and 4, you made use of your checklist to discover your son's or daughter's abilities and learning needs prior to selecting your teaching goals. At this stage, therefore, we hope that you are convinced of the value of some form of recording. In this chapter we intend to re-emphasise its importance, and suggest ways in which it might be done.

Because behaviour is complex, and because changes may be occurring only gradually, you must acquire the habit of keeping periodic checks on progress. Although it is easy to 'see' what we have come to expect, some changes may go unnoticed. Some parents have reported, for example, their delight at being informed by relatives who have not seen their sons or daughters for a year or so of the great progress they have seen during this period. Clearly, the principle is a familiar one. We receive regular bank statements, and adjust our spending accordingly. We may be watching calories, and are happy to complete our weekly weight sheet in order to see whether our appetite control has been rewarded.

Many of you may have chosen teaching objectives which involve not simply the development of a new ability, but an attempt to increase the use to which it is put. In keeping records, therefore, you will sometimes need to count how often behaviour occurs in a given period of time. Similarly you may want to show that a given activity, with practice, can be carried out more quickly than when it was being learned. This involves keeping a record of *how long* it takes to complete the activity (for example, dressing, washing, selecting a correct telephone number).

We do not want the task of keeping records to be seen as too technical. However, we would strongly advise that it is not enough merely to keep a diary. We are going to suggest that you should plot a simple graph as a means of showing how your son or daughter is learning or applying a new ability over a period of time. In the previous two chapters you were told how to make your own 'work book'. In this you practised writing down each goal in clear language. In writing out a goal, you took care to describe what your son or daughter would be doing when training had been successfully completed. In the last chapter, you practised breaking a task down into its successive stages and writing the steps down as a continuous list. It is the steps in this list which will form one side, the vertical part, of our graph for recording progress. Let us look at an example below: (Figure 7.)

The marks along the horizontal part of the graph (labelled Occasions 1 to 20), may refer to whatever intervals, such as hours, days, or weeks, elapse between training sessions. You will recall that we recommended setting objectives which may be attained within a short period, such as a week. In this example, it can be seen that the individual began to make progress most rapidly after the fourth attempt to complete the whole task. How is a graph like this plotted?

Note that the actions involved in carrying out the tasks are written in ascending order alongside the vertical part of the graph. In this example there are 23 steps altogether. Once the individual has been shown how to perform the complete task (has had it demonstrated to him), he is invited to try it himself. He thus begins his first attempt corresponding to the first mark on the horizontal, read from left to right. At the first point of difficulty, where either an error is made or a prompt is required, stop the task and place a cross next to the step reached, placing the cross above the first mark on the horizontal line. This only takes a moment, and whilst marking the graph in this way you should be pointing out what should have been done. You might say, for example, 'That was a good try. Look, you have got as far as here. Let me show you the next step and then you can try again.' The

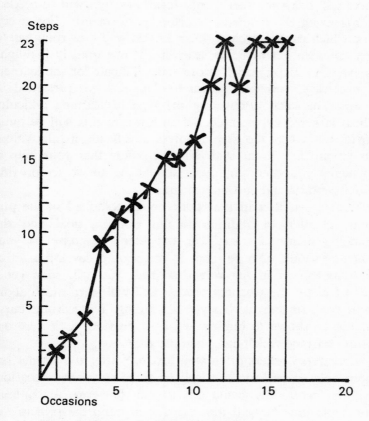

Figure 7. Sample Graph for Recording Progress.

learner should then recommence the task from the beginning. Once again note how far he or she progresses before the first error occurs, or no further progress can be made. Record this position with a second cross, opposite the step reached and above the second mark on the horizontal.

We call a graph like this 'a learning curve'. The quicker your son or daughter learns a particular task the steeper the curve will rise – in other words, fewer attempts will be needed in achieving a complete, errorless performance. For every task which can be broken down in this way a learning curve is a valuable aid to better teaching. It can quickly highlight the step, or steps, which prove most difficult for the learner. If necessary, you may return to the questions presented in Chapter 2, when discovering the type of learning difficulty which is being experienced. Often however this will be quite obvious – when the step involves a difficult manipulation, for example. It is at such difficult points that your help is particularly needed, and you should be quick to provide suitable praise and encouragement.

We suggest that in the 'work book' described in the previous chapter, in addition to the teaching goal and the teaching plan, your son's or daughter's response to your teaching should also be filed. If you should develop a set of learning curves in the way described, you will soon get a good feel for the teaching process and will learn much about your son's or daughter's style of learning. The learning curve should be shown to him or her, as it provides a clear record of the learning which has taken place.

Research workers often stop teaching after the learner has been able to perform the task on three successive occasions without error. We would advise you, however, to continue for some time beyond this, bearing in mind the principle of 'overlearning' mentioned in the previous chapter.

Not all the objectives you have selected for teaching will lend themselves to this kind of recording. You may, for example, simply wish to encourage your son or daughter to smile naturally and easily when smiled at. Whilst this is an important piece of behaviour, it can hardly be broken down into a list of stages. In such a case, you may sit side by side with him or her before a mirror, providing an opportunity for your own smile to be imitated. The record of your teaching might look something like that shown in the figure below.

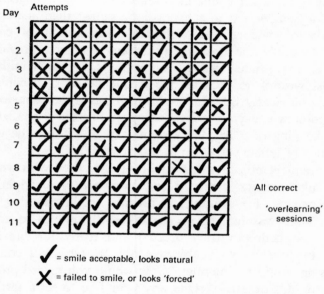

✓ = smile acceptable, looks natural

✗ = failed to smile, or looks 'forced'

Figure 8. Sample Chart for Recording Progress.

As you can see, each individual attempt is marked with a tick, or a cross. Ten attempts are given on each day, and the pattern of ticks and crosses, over successive days, gives an indication of the individual's improved ability to imitate a smile. Of course the next important thing to do, after day six for example, would be to keep a record of how often the individual returned a smile appropriately when the smile came from a different member of the family. In other words, the new ability to smile should be tested outside of the teaching situation, when a mirror was being used and praise was given for a correct performance.

You will no doubt be able to think of other kinds of behaviour which occur with great frequency during the day. The recording of such behaviour would involve a daily count. Smiling was one example. Another is the spontaneous use of conversation. If your objective is to increase conversational ability, you might count the number of times that your son or daughter *begins* a conversation, rather than merely responds to someone else's initiative. You would, of course, need to apply the teaching principles described previously, giving appropriate rewards, for example, for such initiative. Whilst wishing to increase the frequency of such conversations, you clearly would not wish to increase the behaviour to the point where your son or daughter became a chatterbox. The keeping of a frequency count can thus serve the useful function of telling you when to *stop* training!

A frequent objective is to build up the speed with which a particular activity is carried out. Your son or daughter may be very slow, for example, in dressing in the morning. Suppose, after washing, he or she takes 40 minutes to emerge from the bedroom fully dressed and ready for breakfast. You might state your objective as: 'He/she will complete dressing within ten minutes.' How would you record progress towards this objective? One way would be to set a target on each successive day, requiring that two minutes less should be taken than the day before.

Make out a chart over a period of three to four weeks, showing on the vertical part of the chart the time taken at present – marking off the vertical in two-minute intervals down to ten minutes. Note that you should make some provision for the time taken actually to increase on some occasions. In keeping the record, simply record the time taken for dressing on each successive day, praising him or her whenever the target for the day is reached. Experience will show you what is reasonable to set as a daily improvement target – you might complete training in less time than you expect.

In some situations, it is important to note just when certain behaviour occurs. You may wish to spot a pattern, to discover whether the time of the day has any influence on the behaviour, for example. Let us suppose that your son or daughter gets irritable from time to time. In your records, you could break the day down into half-hour intervals, from 8.00am to 10.00pm. Whenever any irritability occurs, simply put a tick in the interval corresponding to that particular time of day. Over successive days, you may spot a pattern building up. The irritability may mostly take place in the afternoon, for example, or before mealtimes. Our brains are not able easily to spot patterns like these over time, but once they are visually recorded they become clear.

So far, we have described charts, graphs and checklists, which aim to show you, as the teacher, how you are doing. In each case of course you should also attempt to make use of the record as a means of showing your son or daughter how the behaviour or ability is improving. But we must remember that fullest possible involvement in the teaching process requires that he or she should receive special consideration in terms of feedback, and encouragement. We will now go on to describe recording systems geared to this end.

Keeping Records Which are Understandable to the Mentally Handicapped Person

The most important thing to remember is that we are dealing with an adolescent or adult. Generally, therefore, systems used with children by school teachers – such as gold stars – would need to be adapted or modified if they are to be acceptable and effective with an older person. We wish to

E

make two specific suggestions. One is a simple 'Personal Record Card' which may be carried around, and the other is a Wall chart. We will describe each of these, illustrating their use.

1. Personal Record Card

Take a piece of stiff white card, measuring approximately $2\frac{1}{2}''$ x 5''. It should fit conveniently into an inside jacket pocket, or a handbag. In Figure 9 below, we illustrate such a card. As you can see, it carries spaces for up to five goals at a time.

The Personal Record Card should be completed by you following discussion with your son or daughter at the end of each day. Only if the behaviour required within a particular teaching goal has been completely satisfactory, meeting the target for that day, should the appropriate square be coloured in. Although up to five goals are shown on the card, we suggest that you should generally work with three, or less, at a time. This card is the property of your son or daughter. It is his or her private record of progress. It may be referred to at any time and it should be understood that the more squares that are coloured in the better overall performance has been. You may enter into a 'contract', agreeing to provide some kind of treat once all the squares have been coloured in.

Research has shown that this private, more adult, personal record can be an effective and acceptable system in practice. The goals which are listed upon it have been mutually chosen, and so also has the treat which will reward progress. The card can become identified with the task itself, resulting in less need for frequent social rewards, such as 'Well done' during training.

Date							
Goal	How I'm doing						
	M	T	W	Th	F	S	Sun
1.							
2.							
3.							
4.							
5.							

Figure 9. 'Personal Record Card'.

2. The Wall Chart

We suggest that you make use of a 'Year Planner' as the basis of this Wall Chart. Once again, the chart is for the benefit of your son or daughter and should therefore be in their possession – mounted on the bedroom wall, for example. Because it shows the month and days, the chart provides a useful means of plotting long-term teaching goals as well as events which are significant in the individual's life. If your son or daughter cannot read, we suggest that symbols or pictures be used to indicate events. We strongly believe, however, that the written word should also accompany such pictures as it is by such pairing together that reading skills will be developed. Let us consider some examples of the chart's use.

Figure 10. Wall Chart.

In helping the individual to develop a sense of identity, his/her birthday should be clearly marked, together with those of other members of the immediate family and closest friends. If a particular event happens regularly, for example, attendance at the Youth Club every Thursday evening, then this should be shown by shading in every Thursday evening throughout the year. This can help to give some sense of perspective, showing how the annual subscription is spread out over evenings, for example. The date of the family holiday can be shown, making it possible to count how many weeks must be waited until that time.

In connection with the development of decision-making skills, specific dates may be marked on the chart on which your son or daughter can decide where the family will go for evening entertainment, or which television programme should be viewed. This use of the chart has already been mentioned in connection with the elimination of problem behaviour, Case No. 1 in Chapter 6.

You may find it possible to link up the Personal Record Card with the Wall Chart. Suppose, for example, that a weekly review is carried out each Sunday. Depending upon performance, there may be a special treat, negotiated in advance. On the Wall Chart, it would be possible to show the weeks in which the special treat was earned by placing an appropriate symbol (for example, a smiling face) in the Sunday of that particular week. Your son or daughter could then count up the total number of such weeks, throughout the year. Has it been a good year? How did it compare with last year? Remember, learning must be fun, and half of that fun must be in recording and celebrating successes.

Although the Personal Record Card and the Wall Chart are the property of your son or daughter, you should take the responsibility for their proper use. Whenever a difficulty occurs, you should discuss this together, modifying the objectives to be worked towards, or the time scale, or the nature of records, as necessary. Never underestimate what may be achieved, and be sure to allow your son or daughter to do some goal setting of their own. Only by such experience will he or she learn to become more realistic about themselves, recognising their strengths as well as their limitations.

8 Activities and exercises 1 – self-help skills

Introduction

So far you have been concerned with considering learning difficulties in assessing the coping behaviour of your son or daughter. You may already have selected several goals which you would like to work on, and with the aid of Chapter 6 have already developed some teaching plans.

In this Section of the book, consisting of three chapters, we will be concerned to present examples of exercises which you may wish to follow. The chapters deal with the self help, social academic and interpersonal skills which are included in the scale in Chapter 3. You should regard these three chapters as resource material for you to use. You will see that the activities suggested are numbered consecutively throughout the whole Section. Exercises are grouped under the same thirty-six headings as used in the scale.

Whilst covering the various levels of each skill, a particular group of exercises intends to suggest a range of alternative approaches. You should feel free to select whichever appear to be most relevant to the specific teaching objective(s) you have selected on the basis of your assessment scale.

Through the exercises we hope to enable your son or daughter to cope by him or herself as much as possible. Part of the definition of 'coping', however, is more difficult to achieve, and that is behaving in a way which is acceptable to others. These two aspects of coping behaviour may best be illustrated by an example: a person may be taught to feed himself so that he can do this without assistance, but to be able to cope in the full sense he should develop table manners which will enable him to eat in public places without drawing undue attention to himself. In devising the exercises, we have taken these two aspects into account.

In order to help you to locate suitable exercises, we provide a chart below which represents the scale items the number of the corresponding exercises, and the pages on which these appear. We would encourage you to devise your own exercises along similar lines.

Scale Item	*Exercises*	*Page numbers*
Chapter 8		
1. Selection of Clothing	1-12	141-143
2. Undressing/Dressing	13-19	143-144
3. Use of Toilet	20-27	144-146
4. Personal Hygiene	28-39	146-147
5. Grooming and Appearance	40-46	148
6. Care of Clothing	47-53	148-150
7. Food and Drink Preparation	54-63	150-151
8. Setting (and Clearing) Table	64-67	151-152
9. Table Habits	68-74	152-153
10. Washing Up	75-79	153
11. Making the Bed	80-83	153-154
12. Tidying Room	84-91	154-155
13. Leisure At Home	92-97	155-156
14. First Aid and Health	98-113	156-158
15. Community Knowledge	114-122	158-160
16. Local Transport	123-130	161-162
17. Shopping	131-138	162-164
18. Eating Out	139-144	164-165
Chapter 9		
19. Communication	145-153	167-169
20. Reading	154-162	169-170
21. Writing	163-169	171-172
22. Number	170-174	172-173
23. Use of Number	175-181	174-175
24. Telling the Time	182-187	176-178

Self-Help Skills

In this chapter we are concerned with self-help skills. These may be thought of as the basic skills that an individual must acquire in order to care for and maintain himself, both at home and in the community. These also include skills which allow a person to seek out and use community resources. You should already be fairly familiar with the self-help skills which we would like to consider with you. They appear as items 1-18 in the assessment scale.

The importance of self-help skills to the daily functioning of an individual cannot be overstated. However, we know that many mentally handicapped individuals lack even these basic skills. If we refer back to Chapter 1, to the table on the educational and social attainments of individuals attending Adult Training Centres, it is clear that much attention needs to be devoted to this area.

For example, the table shows that only 23 per cent of

E*

trainees attending Adult Training Centres are able to prepare a basic meal, including shopping for the necessary ingredients. Just over 50 per cent are said to attend to their personal hygiene. Approximately 80 percent of trainees apparently lack the ability to make use of services in the community, such as medical, dental, or post office. And only 28 per cent of trainees are said to be able to use public transport on their own.

It is encouraging that much more attention is now being given to the development of self-help skills within training programmes. We found in the survey of Adult Training Centres that virtually all centres include attention to personal hygiene within their social training programme. In fact, the staff ranked this item as having the highest priority for training. The majority of centres also provide training in domestic independent living skills, for example housekeeping and cooking. And there is a good deal of evidence that training programmes are beginning to make use of the community as a learning resource, going out on visits to carry out practical exercises, such as shopping.

Whilst training programmes may suffer at times from lack of staff, the survey showed that centres intended, if an extra member of staff were to be recruited, to make the development of social training programmes their highest priority.

We know from our own work with parents that many of these same self-help areas are of concern, especially to older parents. Thus we have purposefully devoted the largest part of this Section to these skills, and to practical exercises for you to try out with your son or daughter. One general point, both in this chapter and the two that follow, is that the exercises should help your son or daughter to attend selectively to certain relevant aspects of the environment.

The importance of this skill may be seen in the following situation.

Have you ever had the experience of walking along in deep thought, when a well known acquaintance breaks in with 'All right then, be like that, don't say hello'. We smile, and apologise. We did not mean to be rude, it was simply our brain protecting our thought processes by switching our attention from other competing impressions and stimuli. In a more extreme case, one of the authors walked a short journey to a destination which could have been reached by two alternative routes. On arriving, deep in thought, it was found impossible to recall which route had been taken! We are only recently becoming clearer in our understanding of how the brain manages to 'switch off' external stimuli in this way.

We know that *important* information is allowed to penetrate through to intrude upon our thoughts. The interesting thing is that it is not the loudness of such information, it is the importance which it signifies for us that matters. It is well known, for example, that a sleeping mother will not be disturbed by a roaring motorbike, but will be roused by the faint cry of her baby in the next room. Similarly, if we are engaged in conversation with one group and our name is mentioned by someone talking in an adjoining group, we 'prick up our ears' and glance in that direction.

These examples serve to illustrate an important aspect of our mastery of our environment – our ability to attend selectively to it. It is just this mastery which is incomplete in the case of many mentally handicapped individuals. For this reason, if we are to help them to cope more effectively in the community we must try to help them develop this ability.

You may recall from Chapter 2 that the first part of the learning process to cause difficulty is often attention to the relevant 'cue'. This point was developed further in Chapter 6. We suggest, therefore, that one type of exercise that you might carry out very early on would aim to help your son or daughter to increase his or her awareness of surroundings. Skills of observation and ability to spot relationships are important for problem solving, for example.

A good game to play in sharpening skills of observation involves recalling as many objects as possible from a set of about 20 placed on a table for this purpose. This game resembles that played at the end of the 'Generation Game' but without the moving conveyor belt. Note what is recalled – how much has this been influenced by such things as: ability to name items, interest in the particular objects, features of the object itself, such as colour or size. Interests identified in this way may prove useful afterwards as rewards for progress.

From this exercise we want to discover whether the individual has become more observant in everyday matters. One useful way of testing this, which includes a check on whether such observations can be put to good use, may be seen in the following exercises:

At a certain point in the morning, whilst travelling with your son or daughter, make a point of saying 'We must telephone ―― (the name of a friend or a family member) before we get back. I will need a 2p for the telephone, so I will put this one to one side, in this top pocket, in case I don't have one later.' Some time later, entering a kiosk, say 'Oh dear, I don't seem to have a 2p.' Look at your son or daughter and pause, giving an opportunity for him or her to recall that you previously placed 2p in your top pocket. If he or she fails to recall this, then you yourself should remember, reminding them also. You may devise similar exercises yourself.

The skill of observation may also be tested through problem solving situations. You might again think of several which would enable you to assist your son or daughter's skills of observation. We present three below as examples:

1. In sight of your son or daughter, fill a kettle at the sink and place it on the worktop (if it is an electric kettle), or on the cooker. Then prepare the teapot together with the cups and saucers in readiness for a cup of tea, saying 'There now, the water will soon boil'. Does your

ACTIVITIES AND EXERCISES 1 – SELF-HELP SKILLS   141

son or daughter point out that the kettle has not yet been switched on, or the cooker lit? Better still, does he or she walk across in order to do it?

2. Choose a destination, within walking distance, which is visible from your house. Tell your son or daughter that you are going to walk across there together. Then take a roundabout route to the destination. Does he or she point out that a shorter cut would be possible?

3. Having boiled some eggs place them on the table next to egg cups which are too large or too small. In the background egg cups of the correct size should be visible. Does your son or daughter point out that you have the wrong sized egg cups?

Now that we have considered with you some general points underlying exercises, we use the remainder of the chapter to present examples of exercises relevant to self-help skills. We stress again that the exercises are intended to provide you with ideas. You may use them or adapt them in the light of the goals or objectives chosen for your own son or daughter. You may develop teaching plans around them following the examples described in Chapter 6.

Activities and Exercises

1.   Selection of Clothing

> (1) Ask son/daughter to show you where clothing and shoes are stored in the house. Can he/she show where his/her own clothes and shoes are kept?
>
> (2) Ask son/daughter to put own clothes away after laundering.
>
> (3) Go through your son's/daughter's wardrobe together, discussing various items of clothing. Which items may be worn with each other? Which are appropriate for individual occasions?

Which are suitable for different weather conditions?

(4) Make out a list of things to be kept in mind when choosing clothes to wear each day. Rehearse this together, considering the weather, the activities and so on.

(5) At night, ask son/daughter to select clothing to wear the next day. As each item is selected, discuss the appropriateness of the choices made, relating these to your checklist of things that should be kept in mind.

(6) Ask son/daughter to express likes and dislikes for pictures of clothing of different types. Magazines or catalogues may be used, and pictures of clothing showing different fashions may be cut out. Ask son/daughter to arrange these pictures in order of preference. Obtain his/her views concerning latest fashions; 'This is what I would like most to wear . . . This is what my friends wear . . . This is what people at work wear', etc.

(7) Ask son/daughter to select various items of clothing from his/her wardrobe. Look for a size label on each item, and point out where this is to be found and what it says. Compare sizes of clothes worn by other family members. To show difference in sizes, check labels and also lay items of clothing on top of each other, to show differences in size.

(8) Ask son/daughter to make a chart showing the different sizes of clothes he/she wears. You may help them by sketching out the items of clothes, or cutting out examples from magazines and pasting these to one side of the sheet. The correct size should be entered alongside on the other half of the sheet. Make out a set of cards together

for each individual item of clothing. Each should show the correct size number, for example: skirt, size 12; shirt, collar size 15½; shoes, size 7.

(9) Take these cards with you on shopping trips and ask son/daughter to locate items of clothing from racks which match his/her size. Use this opportunity also to discuss fashion, choice of clothing to suit his/her age and appearance.

(10) When out shopping with son/daughter try to get him/her to identify sizes of clothing without using cards, relying on memory.

(11) Enable him/her to ask for help from a shop assistant in choosing correct sizes. When an actual purchase is intended, son/daughter may be able to practise using the fitting room correctly, subsequently paying for the article himself/herself.

(12) Involve son/daughter in selecting items of clothing as presents for other family members. Ask him/her to check appropriate sizes in advance and to keep this in mind when selecting clothing.

2. Undressing/dressing

(13) Observe son/daughter attempting to remove and put on simple articles of clothing. Note any difficulties. Examine how you do this yourself when dressing, or ask another member of the family to demonstrate. Give hints concerning easier approaches, for example rolling sock before inserting toe, sitting down when pulling on trousers.

(14) Observe son/daughter attempting to remove or put on outer garments with buttons or zips. Note any difficulties, especially the use of finger and thumb. Where necessary, select items of clothing from the wardrobe which have large buttons or

zips and use these for practice before returning to smaller, buttons, zips.

(15) Having selected items of clothing to be worn the next day (exercise 5), ask son/daughter to point to each item in the *order* in which it should be put on. Have any items been missed? Is the sequence sensible?

(16) Observe complete dressing in the morning, noting the sequence and the overall time taken. You may wish to keep a daily record of time taken. Do certain articles of clothing cause difficulties or take a particularly long time to put on? Consider practice with these articles.

(17) Where there are difficulties concerning the sequence of dressing/undressing, sit down with son/daughter and prepare a simple sequence chart, using words or simple sketches of garments. This sequence chart should be followed when dressing or undressing.

(18) Make separate card showing individual articles of clothing. Shuffle these, and ask son/daughter to place them in the agreed dressing or undressing sequence.

(19) After he/she is dressed, ask him/her to stand in front of a full-length mirror and to check whether he/she has dressed properly. Check particularly that clothes are buttoned, zipped, shirts or blouses tucked in, etc. Ask him/her to make an assessment of own appearance in front of the mirror. Do the clothes match? Is the appearance generally neat and tidy?

3. Use of Toilet

(20) Check whether son/daughter knows when needing toilet, especially if occasionally soiling or wetting during the day. If you can detect a need,

from observing his/her behaviour, draw attention to it by asking an appropriate question. Establish regular toileting routine, for example on waking, after meals, before bed.

(21) Run through simple checklist of toilet routine with son/daughter. For example, checking availability of toilet paper (if needed), closing toilet door, raising or lowering toilet seat, adjusting or readjusting clothing, correct use of toilet paper, flushing toilet, ensuring toilet is left clean, washing and drying hands. Check any difficulties, providing opportunity to practise correct behaviour where necessary. For example, a note or sketch on the inside of the toilet door may serve as a reminder to flush the toilet in cases where this is sometimes forgotten.

(22) Ask son/daughter to check that clothing has been adjusted properly, for example by observing self in full-length mirror. Show how checks should be carried out when no mirror is present.

(23) Show daughter how to operate vending machines for sanitary towels or tampons in public toilets. Point out containers for disposal that are found in public toilets and also point out the correct procedure when at home.

(24) Ensure that your son/daughter is aware of the different signs and symbols which indicate where toilets are to be found.

(25) When out in the community, ask son/daughter to point out the toilet. Ask him/her to find the toilet in a restaurant, for example.

(26) Demonstrate the coin mechanism for coin-operated toilets. Point out where to find out which coin is required.

(27) Observe his/her behaviour in public toilets. If a

cubicle is used, ensure that he/she shuts and locks the door. Make sure he/she is aware of how to flush the toilet and also that he/she washes hands after using it. You may need to point out the various facilities available in public toilets for drying of hands. For example, blow dryer, towel on roll, paper towels.

4. *Personal Hygiene*

(28) As a general introduction to the area of personal hygiene, sketch out for your son/daughter a picture of a man or a woman. Include in the figure, hair, facial features, including teeth, etc. Sit down with your son/daughter and ask him/ her to point out the parts of the body that require regular washing. In particular, ensure that hands, hair, teeth and face are labelled as well as the whole body. Discuss with him/her the frequency with which individual parts of the body should be washed. In particular, focus on the need to wash hands after toileting, before meals, the need to cleanse one's face daily and teeth daily. If your daughter wears make-up, stress the importance of daily removal and proper washing.

(29) Ensure that son/daughter knows the correct procedure for washing hands and face. This will include using the correct water temperature, using soap, and proper drying of hands, face. If son/daughter is not familiar with the routine, make out a task analysis and place this by the sink. You may need to sketch out pictures depicting each stage.

(30) Ensure that son/daughter is familiar with the correct procedure for bathing, that is the correct water temperature, the use of soap, etc. Discuss

the frequency with which baths should be taken.

(31) Discuss the use of deodorants, powders, etc. after bathing, and other regular use.

(32) Ask son/daughter to select items needed for cleaning teeth or dentures. Demonstrate the correct brushing technique – the dentist can recommend illustrative leaflets showing why and how teeth should be cleaned.

(33) Accompany son/daughter to regular dental check-up.

(34) Discuss the need for regular brushing, establishing a routine for this. Discuss the types of food which are harmful to teeth.

(35) Refer to earlier discussions (exercise 28) on the frequency with which hair should be washed. Ensure that son/daughter knows the procedure for washing one's hair. Ensure that hair is thoroughly rinsed after shampooing. You may need to demonstrate the procedure, discussing each stage. Ask son/daughter to assemble or point out everything that is required for washing one's hair.

(36) Demonstrate to son/daughter how to comb out hair when wet.

(37) Show son/daughter how to operate hair dryer, paying attention to the on/off switch, and the various settings. Your daughter may need to be shown how to set her hair.

(38) Discuss regular changes of clothing, especially underclothing and socks. Establish a routine for this, checking that it is followed.

(39) Discuss with daughter the hygiene required during menstruation. Ensure that she is aware of proper sanitary precautions, when sanitary materials will require changing and how to dispose of them appropriately.

5. Grooming and Appearance

(40) Ask son/daughter to stand in front of a full-length mirror and to make a general assessment of him/herself. Discuss with him/her how he or she looks. Is hair neat, for example. Is a shave required, are finger nails clean. Discuss the importance of appearance in general.

(41) Show son/daughter how to scrub fingernails and how to clean them. If unable to manage scissors, you may wish to assist. However son/daughter should be made aware of the *need* to care for nails and to ask for assistance if this is required.

(42) Demonstrate the use of a handkerchief, discuss the necessity of using a handkerchief when required, particularly when sneezing. Remind son/daughter to use a handkerchief when necessary.

(43) Demonstrate to son/daughter the techniques of shaving, using either an electric or a safety razor. Check that son/daughter is aware of when shaving is required and check all safety procedures.

(44) Demonstrate to son/daughter how to comb hair, paying particular attention to how to part hair.

(45) Discuss when hair should be combed, for example before going out, after coming in from blowy weather, etc.

(46) Take son/daughter to barber or to hairdresser. Ask hairdresser to explain hair care procedures.

6. Care of Clothing

(47) After son/daughter has undressed, discuss each item of clothing that has been taken off. Which items should go into the laundry basket, which

items can be worn again, and which items need to be hung up.

(48) Show items required for cleaning and polishing shoes. Focus attention on colour of shoe polish, choice of brush and correct procedure. Discuss when shoes require cleaning and observe performance of the task.

(49) Ask son/daughter to check various labels on items of clothing: for example, check which clothes need to be dry cleaned and which can be hand or machine washed.

(50) Explain the use of the iron. Look at an iron, and on separate cards write out the various fabric settings that are listed on the dial. Explain each of these and then match the cards to various items of clothing which consist of those fabrics. Ask son/daughter to identify another item of clothing that is of the same fabric, and then ask him/her to pick out an article for ironing and to set the dial correctly.

(51) Look at various items of clothing, particularly focussing on the labels specifying whether or not the item should be ironed. Draw out on a separate card the symbol which tells you whether an item of clothing should or should not be ironed.

(52) Demonstrate how to set up the ironing board, and also the settings for 'steam' or 'dry' if your iron has these. Demonstrate the procedure for ironing various items of clothing and ask son/daughter to practise. Ensure also that he/she is aware of how to store the iron and ironing board safely.

(53) Go through your son/daughter's wardrobe with him/her. Show how to check clothing for torn seams, frayed areas and buttons missing. Point

out the need to repair clothing and the importance of this to general appearance. Have son/
daughter observe you carrying out simple repairs
and ask him or her to have a try under supervision; for example cutting out a patch of correct
material and size, selection of correct cotton or
thread, threading the needle, sewing, size of
stitch to use, etc.

7. *Food and Drink Preparation*

(54) Ask son/daughter to choose a hot drink and
make this together with you. A task analysis for
making a pot of tea is provided in Chapter 6.
Focus attention on measurement of correct
quantity of tea/coffee, and sugar and milk if
taken. Point out the need for care in handling
boiling or hot liquids.

(55) Have son/daughter look through various magazines and cut out pictures of meals that he/she
would like to prepare at some time. Make a
work book, using these pictures on one side of
the sheet, leaving a blank sheet opposite to
practise writing out the ingredients required for
each, and a possible recipe. Ask him/her to
copy recipes out from a cookery book.

(56) Ask son/daughter to choose a meal to make. If
he/she has difficulty in deciding, look through
various cook books together.

(57) Together make out a list of ingredients required.
Ask son/daughter to select from the cupboard
the items that you already have in the house.
Make out a separate list of ingredients that will
have to be purchased.

(58) Ask son/daughter to gather together all the
necessary ingredients for the chosen meal.

(59) Refer to exercises presented in the next chapter

(exercises 178-180) to enable son/daughter to measure and weigh out the necessary ingredients.

(60) On separate cards, write out each stage in the recipe. Have son/daughter follow each card and then turn it over to show that he/she has completed the instructions.

(61) Point out numbers on the cooker dial, whether gas or electric, and explain the various settings.

(62) Match numbers on cooker dial to the numbers shown in recipes. Show youngster how to set dial in accordance with the number in the recipe book.

(63) Practise using the numbers by asking son/daughter to set the oven whenever you are cooking, asking him/her to follow the numbers set out in the recipes.

8. Setting (and Clearing) Table

(64) You may wish to make use of a 'shadow board' to teach your son/daughter the correct place settings at table. The 'shadow board' is a useful technique in a number of tasks. Take a large sheet of paper, place it in position on the table and place the eating utensils, crockery, etc. in the correct layout. Use a pencil to trace around the items, removing them to leave the outline shape. This outline may then be used by your son or daughter for practising placing the items in the correct position. Gradually erase the outline so that your son/daughter has to rely more and more on memory.

(65) Demonstrate to son/daughter how to clear the table. Point out the necessity of taking care with glasses, and show how much crockery can be carried at any one time.

(66) Point out how to scrape plates in preparation for washing up. (See also the exercises under scale item 10, which refers to washing up.)

(67) Ask son/daughter to clear the tablecloth of crumbs, and to wipe the table where necessary. Ask son/daughter to decide if cloth can be used again: is it stained or crumpled?

9. *Table Habits*

(68) Review with son/daughter pictures of various items of food. Discuss which cutlery is required to eat the individual foods: for example, the need to use both the knife and the fork to cut up meat.

(69) Demonstrate to your son or daughter the correct procedure for eating a meal. Include for example how to hold a knife and a fork, how to cut up food properly, the amount of food to put in one's mouth at any one time, the speed at which to eat, the need to chew food properly and not to chew with mouth open, nor to speak with the mouth full, etc.

(70) Have other family members be particularly alert to acting as models of eating behaviour.

(71) Serve food up in serving bowl. Discuss with son/daughter what constitutes an adequate helping, how to judge if there is enough food for other family members, for example, when serving self from a certain number of potatoes. Each family member should discuss the amount of food he or she takes to help son/daughter in making judgement.

(72) Use opportunities in the home to enable son/daughter to practise pouring liquids into jugs, glasses, cups, etc. Point out when both hands are needed, for example in steadying a heavy teapot,

and where special care should be taken, with hot liquids and breakables.

(73) Let other family members help son/daughter to learn how to be considerate of others at table. For example, place salt in front of him/her so that other members of the family must ask for it to be passed.

(74) Show son/daughter how to pass vegetables, including the serving spoons. Occasionally let him/her be the first to take a helping and then pass the dish on.

10. Washing Up

(75) Ask son/daughter to gather together the material required for washing up.

(76) Ask him/her to prepare items after meal ready for washing up, scraping food from plates, separating cutlery, glasses, etc.

(77) Demonstrate the washing up procedure, paying particular attention to water temperature, amount of washing-up liquid used, and the sequence of washing greasy and non-greasy items.

(78) After washing up, show son/daughter how to dry items, taking special care with knives and glasswear. Show where items are to be stored, how to stack safely, cutlery in correct drawer compartment, etc.

(79) It may be necessary when teaching to label cupboards, possibly using pictures of items which are stored inside.

11. Making the Bed

(80) Demonstrate the sequence for changing the bed. Have son/daughter assist, for example by tucking in one side, putting on pillow cases.

(81) Ask him/her to show you how to do it. Observe

the sequence and whether or not sheets/blankets
are positioned correctly and pulled straight.

(82) Discuss how often beds need changing, differences between sheets, pillowcases, blankets, and bedspreads. Show where to put dirty sheets for washing or laundering.

(83) Demonstrate how to straighten out sheets in the morning. Ask him/her to do this each day, marking out on a chart.

12. Tidying Room

(84) Make a list of various household tools and appliances that son or daughter may be making use of for learning simple domestic skills, especially those relevant to cleaning own room. This will include, for example, a vacuum cleaner, a carpet sweeper, and cleaning materials.

(85) Cut out pictures of the various items you have listed and ask son or daughter which job each of them is used for. Alternatively, ask son/daughter to pick out the picture of the item that, for example, would be required to clean the carpet. Use printed name cards in place of pictures to repeat exercises.

(86) For each appliance, review with son/daughter where the appliance is stored, how to operate it, what care needs to be taken in its use, how to plug it in, and the necessity of putting it back in its proper place when the task is completed.

(87) Give son/daughter responsibility for the maintenance of his or her own room. He or she must then make out a list of the jobs that require attention in the room, for example weekly vacuuming, dusting, etc. Make out a chart showing these tasks, and ask son or daughter to keep a record of progress in completing them.

(88) Demonstrate how to dust, use of various polishes, etc. Ask son/daughter to polish furniture, clean and shine windows.

(89) Encourage son or daughter to choose own decoration, colour scheme, wallpaper pattern, curtains, etc. Show how posters and objects d'art may be fixed to wall without causing damage. You may choose to make a notice board of a suitable material.

(90) Point out the importance of placing heaters in a safe position, away from fabrics, wooden or foam furniture.

(91) Encourage pride in own room, allowing friends into room only if son or daughter has left it tidy.

13. Leisure at Home

(92) Discuss with son/daughter various leisure activities which may be carried out at home. Ask him/her to suggest some.

(93) Make a list of activities, for example listening to music, watching television, painting, modelling. Read out three or four of them and ask son/daughter to choose one to do by self.

(94) Ask son/daughter to choose something to do without prompting – only remind him/her of items on the list if unable to think of anything by self.

(95) Decide on a time when family members follow individual interests, for example Saturday afternoon. Review with son/daughter the interests of others in the family and encourage him/her to follow own interest, not merely to join in with others.

(96) Discuss forthcoming radio/TV programmes and invite son/daughter to state favourite programmes. With family agreement, allocate proportion of such programme decisions to son/

daughter. Check the times and correct channel/
station, possibly entering this on the wall chart
if it is a regular programme series.

(97) Help son/daughter to choose a creative activity/
hobby which will result in some decorative or
useful end product of benefit to self or others in
the family. This may be decided in the light of
forthcoming personal or family events, such as
birthdays.

14. First Aid and Health

(98) On separate cards, using capital letters, write out
the words WARNING, DANGER, POISON,
BEWARE and so on. Also draw the symbol for
poison. Explain that each of these indicates that
care must be taken. Discuss when and where
these various words/symbols may be found.

(99) On journeys in the local area point out any
dangerous situations which are to be found.

(100) Pick out various household medicines, household
chemicals, or gardening chemicals that have
warning signs on them. Discuss with son/daugh-
ter the need to keep those in a safe place and to
take care when using or handling these items.
Explain their use and ask son/daughter to repeat
where they should be kept.

(101) Discuss various situations in the home which
may be potentially dangerous; for example a hot
stove, leaving electric fires on, leaving other
household appliances constantly plugged in,
leaving items on the stairs, a wet floor, and so
on. Point out labels and some items of clothing
which refer to the need to keep them away from
fire or strong heat.

(102) Make a list of the various types of services that
the family may need to contact for various

reasons: for example the dentist, the doctor, the hospital, the fire brigade and so on. Discuss with son/daughter the situations in which these services and others would be required. See if he/she is able to distinguish which service is required for problems concerning teeth, illness, accident and so on.

(103) Refer to exercise 258, which discusses making a personal telephone directory. Ask son/daughter to add to this directory the telephone numbers of the doctor, the dentist, the local hospital and the emergency telephone number for the fire brigade, police, or ambulance.

(104) Discuss with son/daughter how to make an appointment with the doctor, and then ask him/her to repeat the form of words required. Do this for making an emergency telephone call as well. Ensure that son/daughter is able to give full name and address (see exercises under scale item 29).

(105) Discuss with son/daughter the procedure to follow if he/she sustains a cut or a bruise. Discuss the necessity of washing the cut properly and using a plaster, and so on. Show son/daughter where these items are kept in the home.

(106) Allow son/daughter to assist you in taking care of simple injuries sustained by other members of the family.

(107) Discuss the distinction between simple injuries which may be taken care of within the home, and those which may require medical treatment.

(108) Look through magazines with your son/daughter pointing out various items of food, for example meat, vegetables, or snack food. Discuss the importance of individual items of food to a balanced diet.

(109) You may wish to refer to specialist pamphlets, for example those published by the Health Education Council concerned with nutrition. Use these when acquainting your son/daughter with the essentials of a balanced diet.

(110) Make out cards showing various items of food, and ask son/daughter to put the cards into two piles, according to the foods that one should eat as part of the diet to maintain health, and those which are supplementary. Also point out those items of food which can damage the teeth if eaten excessively.

(111) Discuss the importance of maintaining an acceptable weight. Ask son/daughter to weigh himself/herself regularly and to record this weight.

(112) If your son/daughter is on medication, help him/her to become responsible for taking own tablets or medicine. You may consider using the wall chart, or diary, as a means of showing the frequency with which these should be taken.

(113) Require son/daughter to keep a personal record of the medication taken and check this regularly with them.

15. Community Knowledge

(114) Check that your son/daughter is able to state own name, street/road and house number. Can he/she pronounce this clearly, making him/herself understood by others? Should there be any difficulty here, refer to the exercises found under scale item 29 in Chapter 10.

(115) Go for a walk in your local neighbourhood with your son/daughter, point out your street name and various landmarks. You may wish to use the map suggested in Chapter 5 as an aid for your son/daughter to use when finding the way

around. Use the map to point out various routes which may be taken to arrive at the same destination within the locality. Can son/daughter describe in words how he/she would go to the local post office, library, and so on?

(116) Draw up a number of useful journeys which may be made from home, visiting shops and local services together with your son/daughter, commenting upon the landmarks which may be seen. After practising this several times with your son/daughter, ask him/her to make selected journeys unaccompanied – going on shopping errands for you, for example. In some cases you may wish to enlist the help of a friend in checking that your son/daughter can carry out this exercise safely and by a sensible route.

(117) Discuss road safety with son/daughter, focussing especially on the steps involved in crossing the road. Be sure to follow the code of safety, always providing a good example yourself! Practise crossing the road with son/daughter both at quiet and busy times of the day, pointing out the safe places and the procedure to be followed.

(118) It would be useful to point out on the map where the pelican and zebra crossings, for example, are to be found. Discuss how these differ and the correct procedure to be followed.

(119) Make up a matching game for your son/daughter to play with you. On separate cards print out the name of the different types of shops in your local area: for example, butcher, greengrocer, newsagent, chemist, supermarket. Include also the names of commonly used community services, such as the post office, launderette, and so on. Look through magazines and cut out pictures of various shop fronts which match these names.

Play a game with your son/daughter which involves matching the printed names to the actual pictures. You may adapt this as a 'bingo' game.

(120) Draw or cut out pictures of items that would be purchased in the various shops or of services which you might expect to receive from them. This will include, for example, pictures of vegetables, tinned fruit, meat, postage stamps, postal orders, library books, newspapers, photographic films, and so on. Show your son/daughter one card at a time and ask him/her to select the picture of the kind of shop in which this could be bought. Check that he/she can both say the name correctly and also recognise it when printed.

(121) When you are preparing your shopping list, discuss the items with your son/daughter and ask him/her which shop you would buy particular items from. Take him/her with you shopping and point out the names above various shops, asking him/her to read them. There may be other opportunities for this game, such as travelling in the car, when the names and types of various shops passed may be pointed out.

(122) Discuss with son/daughter what should be done if he/she should become lost. Refer back to exercise 114 in which you checked that he/she could state name and address clearly. What sort of person may be approached for help in this situation? Discuss the role of the policeman in such cases, together with other possibilities, for example enquiring in a local shop for directions. Help your son/daughter to ask for directions clearly, practising the forms of words which may be used.

16. Local Transport

(123) Using the map of your local area once again, mark in the local bus stops. Discuss with your son/daughter bus journeys which are made from these local stops. Against the appropriate bus stop write in useful bus numbers, pointing these out to your son/daughter.

(124) Make a drawing of a bus stop sign, showing the various numbers. Explain that if a number is missing from the sign this means that a bus with that number will not stop at that bus stop.

(125) On separate cards write out the destinations of buses travelling on local routes. Ensure that the form of words used corresponds to the notice which appears on the bus front, for example, 'Town Centre', 'Market Place'. Practise saying the destination and ask your son/daughter to match the bus number to a particular destination.

(126) Walk with son/daughter to the nearest bus stop and point out the numbers on the bus stop. Also point out the type of stop, for example a 'Request Stop'. Explain that this means that the bus will stop only if you put your hand out as a signal.

(127) On a wallet card, or in your son's/daughter's diary, list the important bus numbers and destinations for easy reference. You can also indicate the fare to be paid from local stops to particular destinations.

(128) Practise going on bus journeys with your son/daughter, starting with the choice of the correct bus stop, the selection of the required bus (by its number and destination), and signalling for the bus to stop where necessary. Allow your son/daughter to pay the conductor, or driver, or

F

place coins in a machine, whichever system happens to operate. Practise choosing a seat which is not too far from the exit, keeping the ticket in a safe place in case it needs to be shown. Be sure to keep enough money for the return journey, possibly placing this in a separate pocket for this purpose. Look out for the correct alighting stop, allowing son/daughter to practise judging when to rise and move towards the exit, pressing the bell once to signal the wish to alight.

(129) Allow son/daughter to embark upon a bus journey alone, possibly arranging for a friend or relative to meet them at the destination. Explain to son/daughter that the conductor or driver can offer help when needed, for example in telling him/her where to get off.

(130) You could carry out exercises at home which simulate the paying of a bus fare. Refer to the exercises wall chart items 26 and 27 in the next chapter, which are concerned with money and the use of money, and ensure that son/daughter is familiar with the coinage required when paying the fare and receiving the change. Particular attention may be paid to the provision of the correct fare in the case of buses operated by a driver only.

17. Shopping

(131) Take various items of food out of the cupboard and discuss with son/daughter what each one is and its name. Point out the label on the packet or container and if convenient open in order to show the contents. In order to help son/daughter to become more familiar with the names of items, you may consider making a list of commonly used items and fixing this on the inside of

the cupboard door. Each time you require one of the items in the cupboard you can use this as an opportunity to ask son/daughter to locate the item, find its name on the list, and put a tick next to it.

(132) Print the names of the various food items on cards. Give these cards to son/daughter and ask him/her to pick out food packets or tins from the cupboard and match these to the names of the cards.

(133) Make out a mock shopping list, consisting of some items already discussed in exercises 131 and 132. Tell son/daughter that you are going to pretend that he/she is going on a shopping trip for you. Ask him/her to get the items on the list from the cupboard. As each item is located ask son/daughter to say its name clearly, just as he/she would need to do when asking for it in a shop.

(134) Make out a real shopping list and take son/daughter shopping with you. Give him/her the list and tick off items as they are taken from the shelves or assembled by the shopkeeper.

(135) Let son/daughter practise going to a shop with the list unaccompanied. In preparation for this refer to exercises 119, 120 and 121 concerned with the recognition of different types of shops and also the use of money.

(136) Take son/daughter to other types of shops, pointing out the difference between shops which are self-service and those which are not.

(137) Discuss with son/daughter the appropriate words to use when seeking help from the shop assistant: for example 'Could you please tell me where the sugar is?' . . . 'Please could I have $\frac{1}{2}$lb. of ham?' Devise a role-playing situation

in which you act as a shopkeeper and your son/daughter comes in and asks for various items.

(138) Refer to exercises numbered 1-12 concerned with selection of clothing, particularly size. Accompany son or daughter to various clothing shops, pointing out how to recognise appropriate departments, how to use the store directory, how to locate the appropriate racks with his/her size of clothing.

18. Eating Out

(139) Discuss with son/daughter how to tell the difference between a waiter-service and a self-service restaurant: for example a sign which specifies this, a counter, the presence of waitresses or waiters or a till at the end of a long counter. Use other opportunities to increase your son/daughter's awareness of the different types of restaurant, for example pointing these out when passing cafeterias or restaurants in the local area, and pointing them out as they appear on television.

(140) Demonstrate the use of the self-service restaurant to your son/daughter. Ask him/her to do exactly what you do (whilst allowing choice in selection of the meal!) Show son/daughter where cutlery is kept, etc.

(141) Make out various sample menus, asking son/daughter to select the meal that he/she would like to order. Practise with him/her actually asking for something from the 'menu'.

(142) When passing various restaurants, look at the menu which appears in the window and use this opportunity to discuss with son/daughter the various items of food that he/she would like to

order if you were to be eating in that restaurant. Also discuss prices.

(143) Practise correct table manners in the home and stress to son/daughter the importance of observing these when eating out.

(144) Take son/daughter out for a meal, allowing him/her to practise ordering from the menu, locating the pay desk, etc.

9 Activities and exercises 2 – social academic skills

Closely related to the self-help skills which we considered in the last chapter, are another set of skills which we refer to as 'social academic skills'. These are aspects of the more traditional educational or academic skills, geared to functioning in the community: you will recall that a list of social academic skills appeared in Table 2 in Chapter 3.

Our experience has shown us that attainments in this area, as in that of self-help skills, are urgently in need of assessment and development. Our survey of ATCs showed that approximately 40 per cent of the trainees were unable to count, measure, read, tell the time, use money or write. Many trainees were unable even to sign their own names. As was the case in the self-help area of training, further education programmes are now being developed within Adult Training Centres. The majority of Centres include within their curriculum the use of money, telling the time, counting, recognition and identification of colours, recognition of the written word, comprehension of the written word, simple addition, reading and writing.

You will recall that in the previous chapter we said that we were concerned not only with the development of basic skills which could be used in the home, but in the development of these skills to the point where they could also be used in the community. In the same way we will, for example, be interested in the extension of the skill of telling the time into that of reading time-tables in bus stations and in train stations. Our general focus on reading will emphasise the recognition of key words that are required in various community situations. We hope, therefore, that you will find that the following exercises will have a very practical application.

Activities and Exercises

19. Communication

(145) Observe yourself and son/daughter in various family situations. Do you anticipate his/her requests by providing things without him/her having to ask? Make better use of everyday situations to require son/daughter to ask for things. Discuss the appropriate form of words to be used when making a request.

(146) Play various games requiring cooperation and sharing. Require your son/daughter to express needs which arise during the game – 'May I have another card?', . . . 'Now it's my turn', and so on.

(147) Refer to exercise 167, concerned with printing own name and address. Ask son/daughter to read out name and address when printed, practising clear enunciation.

(148) Discuss various situations where you need to give name and address, for example when telephoning in an emergency, when lost, when making enquiries by telephone. Role play these situations and possibly enlist the help of a friend to ask son/daughter for address.

(149) Point out and discuss situations in which one should not give one's name and address, for example to strangers (but see also exercise 122).

(150) Devise various household situations in which son/daughter is asked to follow simple instructions, and observe his/her actions. Check whether he/she is responding to your verbal instructions

or to your gestures. For example, if you say 'Put it there', and are pointing at the same time, then your son/daughter may be responding to either of these forms of communication. Examine a number of such situations, considering the part which your language played, whether it was too difficult, and whether a more simple direct form of words could have been used.

(151) You may have noticed that you find it easier to understand your son/daughter than do strangers. In order to provide most help in improving their clarity of speech, we suggest you make a list of any particular sounds which he/she appears to find it difficult to pronounce, for example the 's' or 'th' or final 'p', sounds. If there appears to be a number of such problems, obtain advice and help from a speech therapist.

If you have a tape recorder available at your home you might prepare a set of cards showing well known objects the names of which involve the sounds which your son/daughter finds it difficult to pronounce. For each card in turn, you could provide a model, pronouncing the word correctly, and then invite your son/daughter to try to imitate you. Tape record the session and listen back to the results together, pointing out improvements and noting where further practice is required.

(152) Use the tape recorder, if available, to record various family members speaking. Ask individuals, for example, to speak louder, softer, to sound angry, speak very quickly, and so on, showing that the voice may be used in various ways. Help son/daughter to interpret own voice and the various ways in which he/she uses it. Point out the appropriate tone of voice for

different situations, for example at a football match and in a public library.

(153) Be alert to different family activities in which you could ask your son/daughter for their opinion. For example, if watching television in the evening, ask questions such as: 'How much did you like that programme?' . . . 'Did you think it was funny?' Get other family members also to express opinions about activities which take place outside the home, for example at the training centre, youth club, and so on.

Make use of opportunities which arise to encourage son/daughter to express personal feelings and to feel more confident in talking about him/herself. You may set the scene for this by occasionally commenting, for example, 'You seem a bit fed up' or 'It's good to see you so happy today'.

20. Reading

(154) Print out the alphabet on a large sheet, using both capitals and small letters. Then print out each letter on a separate card and ask son/daughter to match each of these to the letters on the large sheet.

(155) Read out each letter of the alphabet and then practise saying a letter and asking son/daughter to pull out the card with that particular letter.

(156) Look at books and magazines, pointing to particular letters and asking son/daughter to identify.

(157) On separate cards print out as many different words as you can think of. Include, for example: Danger, Stop, Bus Stop, Exit, Entrance, Gentlemen, Ladies, Open, Closed, No Smoking. Try

F*

also to include community symbols, for example the symbols of the Lady and Gentleman used on toilets. Read each word out to son/daughter and explain where it may be found.

(158) Use opportunities, for example when out in the local area, on family outings, or watching television, to point out the various words which have been practised in exercise 157.

(159) Collect a number of examples of official forms, application forms and so on. Make a card for each commonly used word which is found in such forms, for example: name, address, date of birth, Please Print in Block Capitals, sex, marital status, occupation and so on. Discuss each of these words with your son/daughter and explain what each refers to. Let your son/daughter practise reading out the various words on the forms, telling you what he/she would put in the space provided.

(160) Discuss with son or daughter the various sources of written information, for example, the telephone book for locating telephone numbers, the newspaper for finding job advertisements, menus in windows of restaurants and the yellow pages in the telephone book for sources of services.

(161) Use other opportunities to enable son/daughter to practise reading skills. For example, look at simple recipes in cook books and ask son/daughter to read out the ingredients; list the directions for some simple activity such as making a pot of tea, and ask son/daughter to read the directions and then follow them.

(162) Encourage son/daughter to make use of the local library. Show him/her how to enlist the help of the librarian in selecting books.

21. *Writing*

(163) In order to help your son/daughter to develop basic printing and writing ability, demonstrate first how to hold a pencil/pen, the correct arm position, correct posture and the correct position of the paper. Ask him/her to trace over various shapes, lines and so on which you have already drawn on the sheet of paper.

By a series of shapes, evolve the letters of the alphabet, printing them out and asking son/daughter to trace over them. In addition to printing each letter of the alphabet, write each one in handwriting style. Once again, ask your son/daughter to practise tracing over them. An extension of this exercise involves simply tracing over numerals which you have printed on the paper.

(164) Ask son/daughter to copy letters and numerals, using the space below, for example, rather than merely tracing over them.

(165) On a separate sheet, write out son's/daughter's full name, using the handwriting script practised earlier. Explain that the writing of one's name (as opposed to its printing) is called one's 'signature'. Ask son/daughter to practise signing his/her own name, until a characteristic and consistent style evolves.

(166) Discuss situations in which one's signature may be required, for example at the bottom of an application form. Using some of the examples of forms collected for previous exercises, ask son/daughter to practise applying his/her signature in the appropriate space. Be sure to explain the danger of signing a form without understanding what it says, explaining that the signature

is a way of showing agreement to something.

(167) Print your son's full name and address on a card. Ensure that he/she recognises this, and is able not only to trace over it but also to print it out without a model to copy. Practise this as often as necessary. You may, for example, ask son/daughter to label some personal possessions, serving both to identify them and also to provide a real reason for practising the skill.

(168) With reference to completing forms, list various other items of information which son/daughter may be required to provide, for example: age, date of birth, telephone number, sex, marital status, date, and so on. Proceed as for the previous exercises, asking son/daughter to trace over the information first, then to copy it from a model which you provide, and finally to print it out unaided in the appropriate spaces on blank forms.

(169) Make use of various family situations to enable son/daughter to have an opportunity to practise printing skills. For example, you may have him/her copy out a shopping list, the menu for the evening, a simple recipe, or various family messages.

22. Number

(170) Place up to ten objects in a row on the table and ask son/daughter to point to each in turn, repeating after you the numbers '1', '2', '3', and so on up to '10'. In this way the simple rote counting is made meaningful, not merely an abstract list. Practise this and substitute different objects, making the situation as real as possible. Count the items of cutlery, eggs, and so on.

(171) Ask son/daughter to help you set the table, counting out four knives, four forks, and four spoons, for example. Ask him/her to count this number out of the cutlery drawer and to count aloud when placing them on the table as an extra check.

(172) Use other realistic situations to enable son/ daughter to practise counting, for example: counting records in the record rack, assisting with household tasks which involve handing across specific numbers of items such as nails, apples, and so on. Point out to son/daughter the numbers which appear on the dials of household appliances, for example the cooker or washing machine. In this way introduce the value of recognising numbers when they appear in printed form. Practise asking son/daughter to select particular dial settings according to the meal being cooked, the material being washed, and so on.

(173) Write out numbers 11-50, asking son/daughter to count these with you and practise recognising the numbers when they appear out of sequence. Explain how important this is when recognising the number on the bus stop and matching it to the correct bus, for example.

(174) Explain the idea of fractions as being the number of parts into which a particular object is divided. You may for example draw a circle and show how this can be cut in half, showing the appropriate symbol for $\frac{1}{2}$ on each side of the dividing line. Give an example of a $\frac{1}{4}$ and a $\frac{1}{3}$. Show how these ideas can be useful when dividing a pie evenly between members of the family, for example.

23. Use of Number

(175) To help son/daughter to develop a concept of which of two numbers is the bigger, start by placing a number of objects in separate piles on the table. Label the number of objects in each pile. Ask son/daughter to count out the number of objects in each pile, and then to say this number and identify it from the card which you have printed out. Then ask him/her to say which pile has the biggest number of objects, which the smallest, etc.

(176) In a similar exercise, place a different number of objects on the table but this time in rows. Ask him/her to say which row is the longest, which is the shortest. Again print out the number of objects in each row on a card.

(177) Based on the exercises above, print out various numbers on cards, in order to see whether son/daughter can tell which number is the largest. If this presents any difficulty, take two cards, and count out the number of objects which correspond to the number shown on the card. Again place these in rows or in piles asking son/daughter to go through the procedure of counting out to see which is the largest.

(178) Show son/daughter the numbers on items of kitchen equipment, such as measuring spoons and measuring jugs. Explain how each of these may be used and which objects may be weighed or measured by them. Measure or weigh out various items and ask son/daughter to identify the number which is shown when the object is weighed.

(179) Ask son/daughter to select unopened packets of food from the cupboard and check the weight as

shown on the packet. Then ask him/her to place the packet on the kitchen scale and to check that the weight shown on the packet and the weight shown by the scale match.

(180) Involve son/daughter in helping you to prepare a simple meal, by asking him/her to assist in weighing out various ingredients. Ask him/her to check the amount required with those stated in the recipe.

(181) You may wish to help your son/daughter to use the four rules of number: addition, subtraction, multiplication, and division. In order to reduce the possibility of confusion, as the methods of teaching these rules vary between schools, we suggest that you consult either the teacher in charge of your son/daughter's final class at school, or the teacher-instructor in the Adult Training Centre which your son/daughter may currently be attending. Simple schemes are available which parents may purchase from good book sellers, but again we suggest you seek local advice when selecting these.

Make use of opportunities within the home to allow your son/daughter to practise adding numbers together, taking numbers away, and possibly multiplying, dividing, or sharing. You might also consider allowing him/her to use a pocket calculator as these are now relatively inexpensive and are widely used by many people. Even if you wish your son/daughter to acquire the basic rules of number, a calculator would provide a useful means of checking answers. It is simple to operate and requires little more than an ability to recognise the numbers and the appropriate symbols.

24. *Telling the Time*

(182) Look through the various magazines and point out different types of clocks and watches. Ensure that your son/daughter knows that these are all used for telling the time.

(183) Refer back to exercises 170-174 concerned with number recognition and counting. Select a clock face which carries all the numbers 1 to 12. Placing the minute finger on 12, move the hour hand in turn around the clock face to point to the numbers 2 to 12. At each setting state the time, for example '2 o'clock, 3 o'clock, 4 o'clock . . .'

Ask son/daughter to repeat each of these after you, and then select hourly positions randomly, asking son/daughter to name the hour. In order to develop an association between the clock time and actual events, discuss with son/daughter various household activities and the time of the day at which they occur. For example: breakfast time, the time when father comes home from work, bedtime, and so on.

(184) Using a similar method to exercise 183, go round the clock face setting the time to '$\frac{1}{4}$ past 2, $\frac{1}{4}$ past 3,' and so on. Ask son/daughter to repeat each of these after you and then to say which hour it is $\frac{1}{4}$ past as you set the time randomly. A similar procedure may be followed when dealing with $\frac{1}{2}$ past the hour and $\frac{1}{4}$ to the hour. Once your son/daughter is able to tell you what time is showing on the clock face when you have set it, allow him/her to practise setting a time which you specify. Start once again with the hour, $\frac{1}{2}$ hour and $\frac{1}{4}$ hour.

(185) In conjunction with the clock face which you

have been using, we suggest that you draw a clock face showing all the minutes. Point out that there are sixty minutes in an hour, and that there are five minutes between each of the twelve numbers on the clock face. Help son/daughter to count out the time to the nearest minute for each setting of the clock face which you present to him/her. Having mastered this, ask son/daughter to set the time to the nearest minute on the real clock face for times which you specify.

(186) Show son/daughter how to set an alarm clock. Practise setting it to different times and also setting the alarm. Show that the bell rings when the set time has been reached, pointing out how to turn the alarm off. Ask son/daughter to take the responsibility for setting own alarm clock each evening, but be sure to check this in the initial stages!

(187) Take a sheet of paper and divide it down the middle. On one side write out the numbers in sequence which make up the 24 hour clock, and on the other side draw a clock face opposite each number showing the appropriate setting of the hands. Point out that the setting is the same for 6 o'clock, as for 18.00 hours, for example. You may wish to devise a matching game in order to provide practice in this difficult concept area.

Discuss with son/daughter the various situations in which the 24 hour clock is used, for example bus and train timetables. As a practical exercise, visit a train or bus station, consult the timetable published and ask son/daughter to state the clock face equivalent. Point out that some clocks, for example in stations, do show the time by the 24 hour system and that this makes matching with the 24 hour timetable much easier.

25. Concept of Time

(188) On separate cards write out the name of each day of the week. Go through these with your son/daughter, reading out each name in turn and then checking that he/she is able to repeat this. Starting with Monday, allow him/her to practise reciting the days of the week aloud in the correct sequence. Show each card as that day of the week is named and continue to practise this until son/daughter can recognise each day when its card is shown out of sequence.

Look at a calendar together and note the days of the week printed on the calendar. Ask son/daughter to match each card in turn with the printed day of the week, pointing out that the days of the week repeat themselves every seven days.

(189) In his/her own diary, personal activities may be recorded which take place on particular days of the week. Discuss family activities which take place throughout the week, noting activities which occur on particular days. For example, on Monday, dad has a meeting, Tuesday is Gateway Club. In this way help son/daughter to associate individual days of the week with various household routines and with personal routines.

(190) Make out a chart. On the left-hand side print the words 'Morning', 'Afternoon', 'Evening' and 'Night'. On the right-hand side of the paper list with your son/daughter his/her own activities which take place during these four different periods. Discuss what morning is, pointing out that it means the start of the day, and discuss

significant events which take place in the morning. Proceed in the same manner for afternoon, evening and night. Ask son/daughter to list out in own diary, activities which take place during these different periods. Discuss other family events which take place in these periods.

(191) Look through magazines, selecting pictures of various activities and discuss whether these take place in the morning, afternoon, evening, or night, or cut out pictures from magazines showing activities which take place at different times and ask son/daughter to place these in separate piles according to whether they take place in the morning, afternoon, evening or night. In this way you will be helping him/her to develop a concept of time.

In your discussion of the activities which take place at different times of the day, point out how activities may differ according to the day of the week, particularly at weekend.

(192) On separate cards write out each month of the year. Read each of these aloud with your son/daughter and ask him/her to repeat them in the correct sequence. Practise this until your son/daughter can recognise the name of the month when it is presented on card out of sequence.

(193) Ask son/daughter to look at the calendar with you and to match each card with the name of the month printed on the calendar.

(194) Ask son/daughter to construct his/her own personal calendar, or else make use of the wall chart described in Chapter 7. Before actually filling in the calendar, you could on separate sheets review each month in turn, listing significant events in his/her life, or in the family, which take place in that month: for example,

own birthday, the birthday of other members of the family, the family's summer holidays and other holidays such as Christmas.

(195) Having completed this calendar or wall chart, play a game in which you describe a certain event and ask your son/daughter to tell you in which month, or on what date, the event takes place. In this way, help your son/daughter to make use of the calendar or wall chart as a reference chart and as a means of planning future events.

(196) Discuss the four seasons in the year and the sequence which they follow. For each season in turn discuss the type of weather to be expected, and the various environmental changes, for example buds on the trees, leaves falling, and so on. Discuss clothing which may be worn. You may refer back to exercises 3 and 4 concerned with selection of clothing appropriate to the weather. Associate various family activities with individual seasons, for example family holidays, gardening tasks, preparation for Christmas, and so on.

(197) Write out the name of each season on a card, and by reference to the months shown on the calendar, ask son/daughter to place the seasons in the correct order.

(198) Look through magazines/books and ask son/daughter to identify the seasons which appear to be depicted there. Try to make use of other situations in which to discuss the season, for example whilst watching television, visiting the Art Gallery, and so on.

(199) Discuss with son/daughter the passage of time. Begin with a small period of time, for example, one minute, five minutes and so on. Ask him/her

to estimate when a minute has passed whilst you time it on your watch. You may also try using the kitchen timer when practising the estimation of minutes.

In order to make the estimation of time more relevant, ask son/daughter to estimate how long it would take to carry out routine tasks in the home. Can he/she estimate how long it takes to boil an egg, for example. How long does it take to get to work on the bus, to get home again in the evening, to wash the dishes, and so on.

(200) When planning the evening's television viewing, discuss with son/daughter how long an individual programme will last and relate this to time on the clock face. Can he/she plan an evening's viewing in such a way as to avoid an unnecessary overlap in selected programmes that appear on different channels? Whilst watching a particular programme, ask him/her to estimate how long it has been on.

(201) Discuss the length of a day, reviewing all the activities that have taken place within that day. In order to help your son/daughter to note the passage of time, ask him/her to tick off each day on the calendar before going to bed.

(202) Having asked your son/daughter to estimate how long particular activities will take, ask him/her to carry out one activity and to time it using own watch. Compare this with the time which was estimated and discuss any difference.

26. Money

(203) Place a sheet of paper on the table. Sit down with your son/daughter and on the paper place in turn an example of each coin, from the ½p up to the 50p piece. Place them in a row, naming

them in turn, and when all are in place draw round the outline of each with a sharp pencil. Remove the coins and then write under each outline the name of the coin: '$\frac{1}{2}$p', '1p', '2p', and so on. Now invite your son/daughter to place each coin back in the correct location, noting the difference in size between the coins. As each coin is positioned state the value, ask your son/daughter to repeat it after you, and continue to practise this exercise until he/she is able to select any coin which you name, placing it correctly in position.

Proceed to do the same exercise using notes of different values. Once again draw round the outline, noting any differences in size, paying particular attention to difference in colour. Below each outline write the value of the note and ask your son/daughter to match the note to the shapes and names as before.

(204) Discuss the coins that are needed for different machines: for example the 2p and 10p pieces when using the telephone, the 5p and 10p pieces when using the launderette, and so on. Make use of any opportunity in the community to help son/daughter to practise actually using these coins in such machines.

(205) In order to help son/daughter to understand the equivalence of coins, you could play a game which involves other members of the family. Each person in turn places one particular coin, or note, on the table, and each other person must then place the same, or equivalent, amount on the table. Ensure that your son/daughter learns that 2 x 5p = 10p, 2 x 50p = £1, and so on.

(206) Make out cards which show money equivalence using real money. For example, at the top of one

card tape on a 10p piece, and lower down on the card tape 10 pennies. On a separate card tape on another 10p piece and tape below it two 5p pieces. (Use this same procedure in order to show other money equivalence.) Review each of these with your son/daughter until he/she can identify individual coins and their equivalence without help.

(207) Make out a mock shopping list with your son/daughter, including items which are regularly purchased. Place beside each item the expected price in the shop and ask son/daughter to help you to work out the total amount to be spent. Allow him/her to practise paying you for the total amount and help him/her to count out the money and to check any change which may be required.

(208) Discuss with son/daughter the need to keep money safely, in a purse or wallet, and point out the sensible form in which to carry moderate amounts – not all in small change, for example. Show how one must take care when opening a purse or wallet that coins do not fall out and that strangers cannot too easily see the contents.

27. Use of Money

(209) Enlist the help of local shopkeepers to help your son/daughter to shop for items and to pay for them appropriately, checking change where necessary.

(210) When you are out shopping with your son/daughter retain the receipts for purchases you have made. When at home, as each item is put away in the cupboard tick it off on the receipt noting the cost of each item. Compare the cost of meat, for example, with the cost of vegetables,

individual items of tinned food, and so on. In this way help your son/daughter to get an idea of the relative cost of various types of items.

(211) Retain the receipt obtained from the previous shopping expedition and take this along on a second occasion. Compare the prices of particular items, noting if there has been any change since the previous occasion. Also compare prices of different brands of the same commodity, for example, coffee, tea, biscuits and so on.

(212) From newspapers, magazine and packets, cut out various special offers and discounts. Discuss whether a particular offer is a 'good buy'. Also discuss how such coupons may be used in order to obtain a reduction in the cost of the items.

(213) Discuss with son/daughter the need to budget for various expenses. Make out a list, for example, of the monthly household expenditure. Examples could include rent, electricity, gas, food, and so on. Discuss with son/daughter the need to pay for essential items first. Discuss how much should be allowed for items that may be considered luxuries. How much can be put aside as savings?

On separate cards write out the names of various items of essential monthly expenditure, luxury items, and so on, as suggested above. Then ask son/daughter to place the cards in two piles: those which should be paid for first, and those which should be given second priority.

(214) In order to help son/daughter to acquire the skill of budgeting, ask him/her first of all to plan the expenditure for a single day. Work out together the amount which will be required for

bus fares, for meals and so on. In the evening, ask for an account of the amount of money spent, and on the basis of this estimate likely expenditure for the following day.

(215) Discuss with son/daughter the importance of avoiding debt, and the part which budgeting can play in avoiding this. Relate this also to the need to save up for expensive purchases.

(216) Encourage your son/daughter to save up for desired items. If he/she has not already done so, you may go along together to the bank or post office and open a savings account. Discuss how much can be put away on a regular basis and help your son/daughter to become familiar with the paying in and drawing out procedures. This will provide opportunity to practise signing name and so on. Ensure that he/she has a personal record of these savings, either in the bank book or post office savings book itself, or by making his/her own record.

28. Colour Recognition and Use

(217) Select a colour and ask son/daughter to point out articles in the immediate environment which are the same or nearly the same. Proceed in this way for main colours such as blue, red, yellow, green. As each colour is pointed to and correctly matched, state its name and ask son/daughter to repeat it after you.

Name a colour and ask son/daughter to point to examples of it. Then show different colours asking your son/daughter to name them.

(218) Follow the same procedure as in 217 for less common colours, for example purple, grey, pink, orange.

(219) Ask son/daughter to describe himself/herself

in terms of colour. What is the colour of hair, eyes, articles of clothing?

(220) Whilst walking around your neighbourhood, point out the traffic lights, asking son/daughter to say what the different colours mean. If necessary, point out that when the red light is on the traffic stops. Be sure to point out that when the lights turn green for traffic it is not safe to cross; whereas when the green man shows on the pelican crossing, it is safe.

(221) Go to your son's/daughter's wardrobe with him/her. Pick out various items of clothing, and name the colour together, discussing which items match. Point out which colours may be worn together and which should be avoided. Encourage your son/daughter to state a favourite colour and discuss colours which may suit his/her hair colouring, for example.

10   Activities and exercises 3 – interpersonal skills

Now that we have considered with you in some depth the basic self-help and social academic skills related to independent functioning in the community, we would like to turn our attention to another set of important skills, and these are 'interpersonal skills'. One of the most frequently neglected areas of preparation for independence is the development of an awareness of normal courtesies, and an ability to recognise the social cues which are used in interpersonal relationships. These are the skills which enable a person to enter into meaningful and fulfilling relationships with individuals or groups in the community. In some senses these are the skills which make a person who he is, the skills which he uses in meeting and in dealing with other people. These are the skills which are required in functioning in the social situation – in other words, they relate to the 'social' self.

These skills are much more difficult to identify than are the types of skills which we talked about in the last two chapters. Traditionally, they have been thought to be much more difficult to focus on in a formal learning situation. They are thought to develop spontaneously within the process of growing and developing, and, perhaps more than any other area of skill, they seem to develop through imitation rather than through structured teaching. Try to think back to who taught you how to tell the significance of a smile, and distinguish it from a smirk. Or do you remember being taught what is the appropriate distance to stand from someone to whom you are talking? Almost certainly not. Yet you have somehow learned this. And you will recall that very early on we said that most human behaviour is learned. We also said that for the individual with learning problems, a much more intensive focus is required than for the rest of us. This applies to interpersonal skills as well.

Let us begin by considering what the term 'interpersonal' means. It means 'between persons' and thus refers to the skills required in social situations. Let us think for a moment just how complicated even a simple social interaction can be. Imagine you are walking down the street and you come across someone you know. You stop and have a chat and then proceed along the way. This sounds simple enough, but if we look at exactly what has taken place, we see that even this brief encounter brought into play many skills which have already been learned.

First there was the act of recognising the other person. Then there was eye to eye contact, and the initiation of conversation. There was a decision that conversation would take place and also about when to stop the conversation. A very quick decision was made on how close to stand to the person, whether any affection needed to be displayed, (if it had been someone that you hadn't seen in a long time you may have embraced, for example, but if it was somebody seen just the day before, this would be unlikely). The 'body language' of the other person may well have indicated to you when the interaction was over. Throughout this sequence you were attending to very subtle social cues.

In order to know how to react in a social situation, a person must have a basic awareness of himself, some concept of himself. Self-concept may be seen as consisting of two main aspects, how a person sees himself and what *value* he puts on himself. The professionals would term these 'self-image' and 'self-esteem'.

Much of the research which has explored self-concept has tried to relate this to an individual's behaviour and to his performance. It is known, for example, that people who are low in self-esteem, often exhibit behaviours which are related to helplessness, and to self-rejection. Thus it may be seen that self-concept is related to adjustment.

In much of the self-concept research, people may be asked to describe themselves, or simply to answer the question 'Who am I?' People tend to describe themselves in terms of their family and in terms of family relationships, saying for example 'I am a husband, I am a brother,' etc. People also describe themselves in terms of their job – in fact, in many social situations, this may be the point of introduction. Other factors may also come in: religious identity, for example, or a hobby. We tend to use these same categories when we describe someone else. Just think about the last time that you told your neighbour about someone who was unknown to them. You tend to report first the person's name, whose spouse he/she is, or what relation they are to someone else you know, and what the person does for a living. We all tend to see people in terms of the roles which they play.

Self-esteem on the other hand reflects the worth that a person feels that he has. Self-worth may be based on one's general capabilities, or physical attributes or some other aspect of personality. It has often been said that different societies hold different types of people in different levels of esteem: the self-made man, the athlete, may be much valued in some communities, and little in others. But in addition to the values of the community, the importance of the family to feelings of self-esteem is critical. Throughout this book, we have been stressing the valuable role which you have to play in the development of your son or daughter. It is perhaps in respect of self-concept that you have one of the most crucial roles to play. The self-concept develops within the person in relation to his environment and depends very strongly on how he interprets the opinions and reactions of other people around him. As handicapped individuals tend to have restricted opportunities for the development of self-concept and self-esteem, the role of the family becomes especially critical to them.

Parents, however, may find it difficult to discover exactly how the youngster feels about himself. It is very often difficult for a young person to express his own feelings. In one of the earlier chapters, we reported on some of our own work in developing a 'choice box' for looking at the concept which mildly and moderately retarded youngsters had of themselves as workers. We were interested to know whether the youngster could make a realistic assessment of himself in this capacity. To the surprise of some, we found that youngsters on the whole were very realistic about themselves, not tending to over-emphasise their abilities and well able to adopt the work habits and attitudes demanded of them. The specific areas in which youngsters thought they had improved over the period of the course compared well with the assessment of their occupational supervisors. And this is not an isolated finding; other studies have also shown that mentally handicapped people are able to make an accurate assessment of themselves. Some studies have also shown that mentally handicapped individuals are able to be trained to observe and to rate the progress of other individuals. They have further shown that a youngster tends to rate himself more accurately than he tends to rate other individuals.

The choice box allowed the youngsters to tell us about themselves, without needing to talk. You can see a picture of this box on the next page.

The box consists of a series of seven buttons, each with its own light above it. The youngster is asked a question and given two statements, each representing one end of the scale within which to answer. In our study, we always had the more positive statement on the right, marked by a green strip. A red strip on the left indicated the less positive statement. As an example of how the choice box was used, the young person was asked.

'How much would you like a job?'

Not at all bothered   Want a job very much

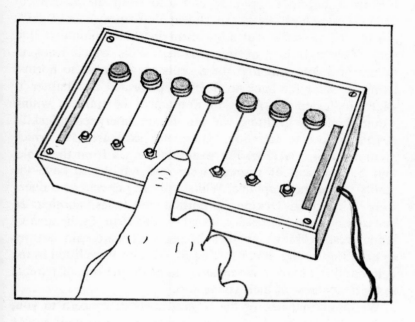

The person administering would say:

'This, the red end, means you are "not at all bothered" and this, the green end, means that "you want a job very much." Put yourself where you think you are.'

During practice items, the youngster's actual answer was interpreted back to him, to ensure that he understood the use of the choice box. Staff who administered this measure found that the youngsters were able to express aspects of their self-concept which they would otherwise have found difficulty in talking about. You may wish to construct your own version of a choice box, for example using a slide with points on it.

Various interpersonal skills will be considered in the exercises at the end of the chapter. You will already be familiar with examples of interpersonal skills, from the table which was presented in Chapter 3, and also from the assessment scale. Research studies have shown that interpersonal skills are related to successful adjustment in the community, that very often it is lack of interpersonal skills which leads to failure at a job, and that these skills are essential to normal living. If we refer back to Table 1 presented in Chapter 1, which indicated the levels of attainment of trainees within Adult Training Centres, we can locate interpersonal skills deserving special attention. These are skill areas in which attainments are lacking. For example, we see from the table, that 55 per cent of trainees were said not yet to have the ability to use the telephone. Whilst only 12 per cent of trainees were said to be lacking in normal courtesies, another 26 per cent had not yet been assessed on this item. In the area of sexual responsibility, another 27 per cent were said not yet to have this ability, but a further 54 per cent were listed in the column 'don't know'. We must stress again the role of parents in the assessment of their youngsters.

We know that one of the biggest areas of concern to you, as to other parents, at the stage of adolescence is your son's/ daughter's sexual development and sexual awareness. Many aspects of this development relate to self-help areas, particularly hygiene, and some of these problems have already been discussed in Chapter 8. However, consideration of sexual development and awareness must necessarily extend beyond matters of hygiene. You will perhaps be wondering if you should encourage your son/daughter to form relationships with members of the opposite sex, whether marriage is a realistic prospect, or whether you should simply ignore the areas of sexual awareness altogether. Some research has shown that mildly handicapped individuals who do marry, make a more successful adjustment than individuals on their own. The partners seem to provide mutual support and companionship and a buffer against difficulties experienced outside. Very often, one member of the partnership is the stronger of the two.

We have considered sex education in the workshop which we have run for parents of mentally handicapped adolescents and adults. These parents seemed to be in general agreement that treatment of this subject really depends on the individual in question, and that it should not be ignored if it is actually brought up by the youngster. Parents agreed that answers should be given to questions as frankly as possible.

It is difficult to provide parents with accurate guidance in this area. What we would like to do is to suggest that parents acquire as much information as possible, so in the appendices we list a number of films and other resources on this subject.

Interpersonal skills are also important in a number of other situations. We found, for example, that lack of such skills was frequently referred to by employers as reasons for failure in employment. Difficulties referred to coping with teasing by co-workers, personality problems, uncooperativeness, communication problems, appearance, leisure, and social acceptability. When staff were asked to list areas in which further training was necessary for individuals to become capable of open or sheltered employment, again we saw that interpersonal skills were frequently mentioned.

In developing the activities or exercises in this chapter, we have taken account of those priority areas, identified both by research and practice.

Activities and Exercises

29. Personal Knowledge

(222) Look through your family photograph album, pausing at photographs in which your son/daughter appears. Print the name of your son/daughter on a card and point to this whenever his/her photo appears. Ask him/her to repeat the name after you.

To help your son/daughter to recognise his/her

name when written down, make out several identification tags to attach to his/her personal
possessions.

(223) Look up your family's surname in the telephone
directory and ask your son/daughter to match
the name written on the card to the names in
the directory. Point out the use of the initial to
discriminate between surnames which are the
same, and also the way in which the address
may be used as an extra check.

(224) Print out the family address on a card. Include
the house number, and the street or road name.
Show son/daughter how the number on the card
matches the number on the front door, for
example. Walk down the street and match the
name of the street written on the card with the
street sign.

As a realistic way of helping your son/daugh-
ter to check the complete address, ask him/her
to gather up the mail each morning, matching
the addresses on it with that printed on the
card.

(225) Print out a number of addresses, for example
those of other relatives and neighbours, and ask
son/daughter to sort through these and pick out
his/her own address.

(226) Refer back to exercise 167 in which your son/
daughter was asked to print the family address.
Ask him/her to make out a card suitable for
carrying in his/her wallet or purse, on which
the full name and address appears.

(227) Print out your telephone number on a card.
Read the numbers aloud to your son/daughter.
Refer back to exercise 223 in which you referred
to the telephone directory, and now read aloud
the number from the card and match it to the

number shown in the directory. Ask son/daughter to note that these two match. Ask him/her to read the number aloud.

(228) In a similar exercise to that carried out with the address, print out the telephone numbers of relatives and friends, as well as your own telephone number, and ask son/daughter to pick out the card with his/her own telephone number on it.

(229) Print out date of birth on a card in two forms: using only numbers, and using the day, the month and the year. Go over this with your son/daughter explaining that these are two ways of writing down his/her own date of birth. Ask him/her to read each of these forms aloud after you. Refer to exercise 168 concerned with completing official forms, and ask him/her to fill in the date of birth in the form required.

(230) Look at a map of the world and locate your own country. Turn to a larger scale map of your country and locate your own city. Discuss with son/daughter his/her nationality and the relationship which this has to birth place. Look at the national flag and compare it with the flags of other nations.

(231) Discuss religion of the family, where appropriate, pointing out that there are other religions and beliefs, possibly relating this to the map of the world.

(232) Consider each member of your family in turn, possibly referring to the family photo album. Ask your son/daughter to name each member of the family, noting the different surnames of cousins, aunts, and so on. Practise describing individuals in the immediate family in terms of their name, age, sex, appearance and role or

occupation. Point out the relationship which each has to your son/daughter, asking him/her to repeat this: for example, older sister, younger brother and so on.

(233) Examine your son's/daughter's leisure time activities. Ask him/her to report on progress being made, and give praise where applicable. Ask him/her to make use of own personal diary to record progress.

(234) Make use of various family activities or personal hobbies of son/daughter to get him/her to assess own strengths and limitations. Before carrying out any activity, ask son/daughter to estimate potential success, for example 'I can swim one length of the pool'. Afterwards, discuss the relative success. Take every opportunity to point out to son/daughter where progress has been made, and new skills acquired. This might also be achieved by sitting down with your son/daughter to review improvements in coping skills since the assessment scale was first completed.

30. Conversation

(235) Carry out role play exercises with your son/daughter, involving other members of the family. Practise greeting behaviour saying 'Hello, how are you, good morning,' and so on.

(236) Practise introducing someone to someone else, for example 'Paul, I would like you to meet Jim. Jim, this is Paul.' Once this has been accomplished make the introductions more helpful, adding, for example 'Jim is one of my friends from school'.

Give your son/daughter opportunities to respond to an introduction of this type. Role play a situation in which he/she can develop appropriate responses such as 'I am pleased to meet you.'

(237) To encourage your son/daughter to relate experiences and recent events, involve each member of the family in recounting the type of day they have had, over the evening meal, for example. Discuss common experiences, for example a visit to the shops, or football match.

Suggest to son/daughter that a scrapbook of events might be kept, including snapshots, theatre programmes, and other souvenirs. Use this as a talking point to stimulate discussion.

(238) Ask son/daughter to talk about the interests of different members of the family and of his/her friends. Consider ways in which son/daughter may become better acquainted with the interests of others with whom he/she is in regular contact. Extend this to consider how one might find out the interests of a new acquaintance, asking about their job, hobbies, and so on. Make a list of the people considered and write against each a short account of their interests, perhaps illustrating this by cartoon sketches. Then select an individual and ask your son/daughter to show how they would enter into a conversation and take account of the interests of that other person.

(239) Discuss with your son/daughter situations or occasions in which it might be necessary to ask someone else's advice or opinion. Distinguish between the type of help needed in order to obtain information and that which may be needed in order to understand feelings.

Help son/daughter to realise that people often disagree about things, and that they have a right to their own opinions. This may be illustrated by watching a discussion on the television, or listening to a radio debate. Show how this is also true within the family. Make use of family discussion times to encourage son/daughter to express opinions about issues of common concern.

(240) Role play a situation in which one person shows that he is bored with the conversation of another, for example by yawning, looking away, humming, looking at watch. Point out to son/daughter that these are signs which mean the conversation should be brought to an end soon. Help your son/daughter to learn how to end a conversation politely, for example: 'Well, I must be off now,' and so on.

31. Social Graces

(241) Discuss the use of the words 'please', 'thank you'. Think of situations in which these are appropriate, and the accompanying gesture such as a nod or shake of the head which may accompany them.

Use everyday situations in order to encourage son/daughter to practise using these expressions appropriately.

(242) Refer back to exercise 235, concerned with greeting behaviour, and develop this to illustrate the different forms of greeting which are appropriate when meeting someone whom you see every day, whom you see more than once a day, or whom you see infrequently. Point out the differences between each of these. For example, one does not shake hands with someone who is seen every day, particularly if they are seen more than once in the same day. It is more appropriate to shake hands with someone to whom one is being introduced, or who is seen infrequently. Point out other important aspects of greeting,

the importance of looking at the person to whom you are speaking, the appropriate distance to stand in relation to the person being spoken to. These behaviours need to be practised, particularly if your son/daughter has developed any inappropriate habits related to greeting others.

(243) Use opportunities both within the home and in the community to encourage your son/daughter to become aware of the need to wait his/her turn, or to join a queue. At meal times, for example, you might place your son/daughter next to the person who is serving the meal, passing the plates around before taking his/her own portion. Meal times also provide an opportunity to practise asking for various items to be passed and for saying 'thank you' or 'you're welcome', and so on.

(244) Point out when it is appropriate or necessary to knock on a door before entering. Make out individual cards showing such expressions as: 'please knock', 'knock, then enter', or 'enter please'. Discuss the meaning of each of these expressions and the appropriate response.

Within the home it might be appropriate to knock on the toilet door, or a bedroom door, before entering.

When out in the community with your son/daughter consider the entrances to various public buildings and shops, noting that it is not necessary in most cases to knock upon these doors.

(245) Discuss with son/daughter various circumstances in which one should excuse oneself before leaving, for example, when leaving the table, when leaving a group discussion. It may also be necessary to excuse oneself before interrupting a

conversation, or when someone indicates that they need privacy.

32. Friendships

(246) Try to be aware of instances within the home where cooperation and sharing could be practised. For example, your son/daughter may be able to help you with some of the housework, in preparing meals, or in taking responsibility for tidying his/her own room. You may wish to devise a family washing up rota.

(247) Discuss with son/daughter the difference between lending possessions and giving them to others. Think of examples of items which might be lent to a friend, for example a record, and those which are personal and should not be lent, for example a tooth brush. Devise role play situations by which your son/daughter may learn how to respond appropriately when asked whether something may be borrowed.

(248) Think of situations in which it would be inappropriate to express sympathy and discuss with your son/daughter the form of words which may be used. Use real situations as they arise: sending a 'get well' card, for example.

(249) Suggest to your son/daughter that the wall chart or diary may be used to record the birthdays of family members and friends, serving as a reminder to keep in touch, or send birthday cards or small gifts where appropriate. Praise any initiative which your son/daughter shows in keeping in touch with distant friends or in remembering significant birthdays, Mother's day, and so on, without needing to be reminded.

(250) Help your son/daughter to become sensitive to

the feelings of others by, for example, occasionally informing him/her that you are feeling tired,
or a little unwell. Note whether he/she responds
by offering to help in some way and be ready to
suggest the form of help which would be most
appreciated.

(251) Handicapped people often express a wish to be
of service to others less fortunate, or more
dependent, than themselves. Explore how your
son/daughter feels about this and consider together the possibilities which may exist in your
local area. Contact may be made with one of the
many voluntary groups which operate, providing
meals on wheels, or visiting sick or lonely people.
Social Services Departments and hospitals often
have someone known as the 'voluntary effort
organiser' who can offer advice on such matters.

33. Leisure – Group Activities

(252) Take son/daughter to a public function, such as
the theatre, football match, parish dance, or
concert. Express pleasure at his/her company
and ask whether he/she is enjoying the occasion
also.

(253) Encourage son/daughter to join a club or society
which caters for his/her interests. Help him/her
to develop individual preferences and to choose a
club appropriately. Suggest the value of regular
attendance and of active membership.

(254) Allow son/daughter to experience a range of
leisure activities, both as a spectator and as a
participant. Note that some activities, such as
membership of a cycling or tennis club, can
provide for both social and physical wellbeing.
Fell-walking, for example, can be equally enjoyed
by mentally handicapped and non handicapped

individuals – indeed, intelligence has little to do with stamina and physical strength!

(255) Encourage son/daughter to participate where possible in team activities, experiencing the feelings of pride and loyalty which are associated with team success. The mentally handicapped sports day and inter-Centre soccer league are examples of such opportunities.

(256) Explore any talent which your son/daughter may have for musical appreciation or perform-ance, or possibly for miming, acting, singing or dancing. Help him/her to experience a sense of group membership and its associated bene-fits: participating in a band or choir, for example.

34. Telephone

(257) Refer back to exercises 227, 228 in which your son/daughter practised saying and recognising the family telephone number. Allow him/her to answer the telephone, having practised the correct procedure: saying the telephone number first after lifting the receiver.

Show him/her how to call the appropriate per-son to the phone, how to take a message or deal with a wrong number. If the telephone is not the family phone, show son/daughter that the num-ber to say on answering the phone appears in the centre of the telephone dial. Enlist the help of friends or relatives in giving son/daughter opportunities to apply this.

(258) Involve son/daughter in constructing a personal telephone directory. It may be helpful to include a small photograph of each individual, together with their name, against the telephone numbers. List also emergency services, possibly shown by

an appropriate symbol, with the corresponding telephone number.

(259) With the receiver down, ask son/daughter to practise careful dialling of numbers from their personal telephone directory. Lift the receiver and listen to the dialling tone, pressing the lever or rest where necessary. Allow son/daughter to become familiar with this tone as a pre-requisite for dialling.

Possibly with the help of a relative or friend, arrange a time when son/daughter can dial certain numbers, experiencing the dialling tone or engaged tone, and the giving and receiving of a simple message. Point out the correct position of the receiver, which end to speak into, and the appropriate level of voice to use.

(260) Periodically review with son/daughter the reasons and the correct procedure for making an emergency telephone call. Stress the importance of giving name and the address and telephone number from which he/she is speaking followed by a brief account of the type of emergency.

(261) Take son/daughter to the nearest public telephone booth – point out its characteristic shape and colour. Take along a range of coins, demonstrating which coin to use for a local or more distant call. Select a coin and place it ready in the appropriate slot.

Show son/daughter how to lift the receiver, listen for the dialling tone and then allow him/her to dial a well known number. Listen together for the tone (rapid pips) and then press the coin into the slot when the person responds. Have another coin ready when the pay tone returns, and this time allow son/daughter to place it in the correct slot unaided.

(262) Use the personal telephone directory as a model, and, referring back to exercises 223 and 227 on looking up the family name and telephone number in the directory, help son/daughter to look up the telephone number of a friend or relative. Show how the surname, initial, and address should be used as a guide and a check. You may need to refer back to some of the earlier exercises under heading 20, 'Reading'.

35. Responsibility

(263) Use various family activities and routines to allow your son/daughter to develop a personal sense of responsibility. You may wish to develop certain rules for members of the family to observe: for example the last person to go to bed must check that the doors are locked, turn off the television or similar appliances, and then turn out the light before retiring. Discuss these rules with your son/daughter in the context of safety and general family harmony. Explain, for example, that the chain should be placed on the door before opening it to strangers, especially at night.

Review any rules which may apply at the training centre or at your son's/daughter's place of work. Discuss the reasons for such rules.

(264) The family might set aside part of one evening in the week, after dinner say, as an opportunity to discuss each other's behaviour – a friendly opportunity for each person to say how he/she feels others could improve. Encourage son/daughter to participate in this and to accept justifiable criticism with good humour, as well as to offer it where necessary.

Discuss how an apology should be made and

responded to, and be sure to praise your son/daughter if the behaviour concerned improves.

(265) Encourage your son/daughter to accept responsibility for selecting clothes to wear in the morning. Show your approval of sensible selection and any initiative concerned with care of clothing and the development of personal preferences.

(266) Take your son/daughter to a restaurant and allow him/her to select a meal and place an order – this might be extended to include your son/daughter asking each member of the family what they wish to order, and then placing the order with the waiter when this is being taken. Where appropriate he/she may also place an order for drinks and be shown how to pay for this, and the appropriate amount to leave as a tip.

(267) If you have a pet, a cat or a dog, for example, make son/daughter responsible for feeding the animal on a particular day of the week, then every morning, twice a day, and then for a whole week. Point out the dependence of the animal on the family for its food and the need to be reliable. Point out also the need to keep harmful substances out of reach of the pet, and refer back to exercises 98, 100 concerned with the recognition of such substances.

(268) If possible, designate a certain section of the garden as the responsibility of your son/daughter. Encourage him/her to decide what to plant there, either flowers or vegetables, pointing out the importance of regular watering, feeding the soil, weeding and pruning, and so on.

36. Sexual Knowledge and Behaviour

(269) Discuss with your son/daughter the terms which

are used to refer to the sex of a person, for example, man, woman, boy, girl, uncle, aunt. Consider with him/her the basic differences between the male and female in physical appearance and characteristics, clothing worn, tone of voice, physical strength, likely type of job, and so on. Ensure that son/daughter can identify own sex correctly.

(270) You may wish to make use of books or pamphlets, such as those available from the Health Education Council (the address of which is shown in the Appendix), when discussing with your son/daughter the physical and sexual development which has taken place during adolescence. You may refer back to exercises under heading 4, 'Personal Hygiene'.

If you judge it to be appropriate, you may also make use of such pamphlets to discuss such issues as conception, methods of family planning, and childbirth with your son/daughter. Dealing with these questions when they arise, within the context of the family and marriage, can help your son/daughter to develop appropriate attitudes and an understanding of the family's role within society.

(271) Point out that the changes during adolescence are signs of becoming an adult, and that this brings with it both greater opportunities and greater responsibilities. Give examples of ways in which you yourself have come to expect more from your son/daughter since he/she has achieved adulthood.

(272) Discuss the significance of displays of affection and how these differ between children and adults. Discuss how one should behave when with

friends of either sex and appropriate/inappropriate displays of affection.

We suggest that you discuss these matters with parents of other handicapped people of a similar age and also with professionals who may be working with them on a daily basis. Should your son/daughter form a close and long-term relationship, beyond merely having a girlfriend/boyfriend, discussion on the feasibility of marriage will inevitably arise. Review your son's/daughter's progress and ability to cope, and consider his/her strengths and dependences in the context of those of the prospective partner. With help and support many mentally handicapped individuals have shown themselves to be capable of stable and satisfying marriages and long term friendships, and your son/daughter may be one who could achieve this with your support and that of appropriate professionals. We feel that you would want to explore this matter as fully as possible.

11 Reviewing progress

Let us now pause to take stock of what has been achieved. If you have kept regular records, you will already have a clear idea about the areas of ability which are showing improvement, or otherwise. You will be able to evaluate the success of your teaching plans, and to make improvements where necessary. You may find that new objectives should now be selected, new resources gathered together, or different teaching strategies tried.

Above all, it is important to keep a sense of perspective, to try to keep in view the overall needs of your son/daughter as a person. Similarly, the needs of the rest of the family must be considered. Not only will these considerations have a possible influence upon the teaching objectives selected, they may also influence your allocation of time, and possibly the selection of rewards to use. A younger brother or sister, for example, may feel it unfair if the special treats which are provided for your mentally handicapped son/daughter are not matched by similar treats or recognition for the progress made by others in the family.

At this stage, you need to know whether your son/daughter, having developed new abilities, can apply them in a new setting, or combine them with other abilities when carrying out a realistic exercise intended to test their ability to cope.

We suggest that you carry out such a review at approximately six monthly intervals. Return to the chart for assessing coping skills, previously completed in pencil, and complete it a second time. You might use a plus sign, instead of a tick, on this second occasion. Look back through your workbook, especially at your teaching plans and the records you kept. Is there any evidence that your son/daughter is responding more rapidly to your teaching efforts? You should look for a possible acceleration in the steepness of the learning curves.

Look back through the lists of resources which you have used, you may spot that certain resources have been particularly useful in a number of different teaching plans. In particular, note the various people who have been involved, from time to time, in implementing the plans. You may discover that a certain member of the family, an aunt, or grandparent, emerges as a particularly powerful ally. On the other hand, if overall progress has been slow, do not be discouraged, consider whether the teaching steps were too large. Maybe there is some behaviour which, whilst not being regarded as 'problem behaviour', is found to need some modification or improvement if more effective learning is to take place: you may decide, for example, that a new objective would be to increase the period of time during which your son/daughter is able to attend to a given task before losing concentration.

As suggested in Chapter 4, when discussing Figure 5, we expect that you will want to help your son/daughter to consolidate the knowledge and abilities already gained. It seems sensible to help him/her to be able to carry out certain things unaided which at present still need some supervision or prompting. You now need to discover whether your son/daughter has remembered what has been taught, has the confidence to apply this, and can carry it out successfully outside the protected environment of the home. This ability to 'transfer' learning to new situations is a crucial test of the real effectiveness of the teaching plan. You will recall that teaching should always include consideration of ways in which opportunities may be provided for the particular skill to be practised.

Consider ways in which individual exercises may be strung together to produce a more rigorous test of ability to cope.

In fact you might describe this process as 'getting it together'. Let us consider some examples:

Ask your son/daughter to invite a friend over for tea. He/she should telephone in order to give directions on how to get to the house, giving the number of the bus and indicating the correct alighting stop by reference to some suitable landmark. Your son/daughter should then begin to prepare a simple meal, estimating the time which would be required for this, setting the table and having all preparations completed by the time the friend arrives, show appropriate greeting behaviour and introduce him/her to members of the family. After the meal, he/she might again help you by washing the dishes. In this example, you can see that many individual exercises have been brought together.

On another occasion. you might accompany your son/daughter on a trip to buy a new suit or a dress. Check whether he/she can find an appropriate shop or the appropriate department in a large store. Allow him/her to select a style and a material, taking account of personal preference and also the amount which can be afforded. Check that your son/daughter informs the sales assistant of his/her correct measurements or sizes, or else requests that such measurements should be taken. Encourage him/her to budget for the purchase of this item, either opening a budget account or using an existing savings account.

A third idea might be to draw up a shopping list of items needed in the home, to be purchased from two or three different kinds of shops. Send your son/daughter on a shopping expedition alone to purchase the items, giving him/her enough money to cover the cost of a return bus journey to the shopping centre and the cost of the items. Require him/her to telephone home from the shopping centre just before setting off on the return journey. Upon return, ask him/her to describe the outing; the number of bus taken, the amount of fare paid, the shops visited, any difficulties which may have been experienced in obtaining items on the list, and the time of setting off for the return journey. Once again, this expedition combines many sub-skills which have been described in the exercises and brings them together in a meaningful and realistic way.

We feel sure that you will agree that if your son or daughter is able to carry out activities of this kind then you can feel much more confident about his or her ability to cope more independently in future years, when the support that you are now able to give may no longer be present. Even though your son or daughter may continue to live with you in the family home for many more years, the sense of achievement which will accompany the ability to contribute to the life of the family will amply justify the help which you are now able to give.

12   Looking at the future

Now that you have read this book to this stage, we would like to consider the implications for the future of what we have been saying. We hope that you will now have come to regard the term 'education' as having a wide application, not restricted to the stage of childhood. In looking at the way in which our services for the mentally handicapped have developed, we can trace a gradual shift from custodial attitudes through to the present full recognition of the right of the individual not only to live *in* the community, but also to contribute to its wellbeing.

There has never been a time of greater awareness of the needs and potential of mentally handicapped individuals. During the present decade, great advances have been made in changing attitudes towards handicap in general. This is reflected in higher levels of expectation on the part of parents, practitioners, and handicapped people themselves about what may be achieved. A sound philosophy is being developed, and it is significantly affecting the type of services which are being offered.

Government policy, outlined in the White Paper *Better Services for the Mentally Handicapped*, has clearly placed the emphasis on a full community-based service to the individual and his family. The *Education (Handicapped Children) Act, 1970,* marked a significant stage in official recognition that all mentally handicapped individuals can benefit from education. This was a great breakthrough, which has more recently led to wider consideration of the implications for the child once he has left school (for example: Warnock, 1978).

In 1977, for the first time, it was possible to learn of the views of staff working with mentally handicapped adults in Adult Training Centres throughout the country. The first National Survey, carried out by the authors, showed that staff were actively questioning their role and recognising the importance of an educational approach to their work. Indeed, it was due to staff initiative, supported by parents, that the National Development Group, set up by the Secretary of State in 1976, produced in the following year Pamphlet Number 5, *Day Services for Mentally Handicapped Adults.* This pamphlet, now a discussion document, is the focus of wide ranging discussions. It will form the basis of a new statement of government policy on such services.

In the light of the above developments you might ask 'What does this all mean for the parents, faced with the day to day problems of a handicapped adolescent or adult in the family?' Basically, it should mean a renewed enthusiasm and a determination to take full advantage of these developments. There is still a good deal to learn and much progress to be made in putting this into practice. In this book, we have attempted to introduce you to the ways in which you, as parents, can make an active contribution.

In this chapter we want to explore this further and to suggest ways in which you can share your experiences with other parents and with professionals. We also attempt to provide you with a better understanding of the overall system of services available. We hope that you will make best use of the options which already exist and play your part in shaping future policy.

One of the dangers which many parents have been aware of, resulting from their commitment to help their handicapped child, has been the possible neglect of other members of the family. This is just one reason for parents to build up a network of support, involving relatives, neighbours and friends. An extensive study, by Michael Bayley, of the needs of families with profoundly handicapped adults living at home, stressed the importance of this as a healthy method of sharing the problems.

In contrast, some parents have attempted to deal with the problems entirely on their own, experiencing a dramatic curtailment of their social life, a loss of friends, and a great restriction of their individual freedom. In the short term, such families may have coped adequately, but in the long term their isolation produced difficulties for their handicapped member, especially as they themselves advanced in age.

In his report on the above study, carried out in Sheffield, Bayley includes extensive quotations from the views expressed by parents. He argues that the official services provided by the Local Authority must become more relevant to the needs of the families, supplementing the support which the family already receives in an informal way. All such official help should ideally be 'regular, reliable, relatively permanent, accessible, acceptable, and whenever possible reciprocal.'

Parents and Professionals in Partnership
We believe it is essential that the collaboration between parents and professionals in the field of mental handicap should become closer. Some progress towards this has already been made, but it is not yet known how much more can be achieved. We know, for example, that many schools keep a teacher-parent diary. This is completed by the teachers during the day, and the parents in the evenings. It provides a two-way communication between the home and the school, helping parents and teachers to focus on the same issues and adopt similar approaches to dealing with them.

There have already been a number of 'workshops' for parents of young mentally handicapped children. These have proved very successful, and served to strengthen and extend the partnership between the parents and teachers in special schools. Workshops for parents of mentally handicapped adolescents and adults, however, are only beginning to be established. The value of such workshops, consisting of a combination of lectures, demonstrations, practical exercises and group discussions, is to enable all who participate to learn a good deal more about the needs of young mentally handicapped adults.

Parents are able to offer each other support and practical advice, and a means of comparing notes about common problems and methods of tackling them. Some of you may find the principles described in this book, together with the exercises suggested, a useful basis for a working link between parents and professionals. When workshops are held in the setting of an educational or training establishment, with the staff closely involved in the work of the groups, then firm foundations can be laid for a long-term partnership between the unit and the home.

Staff on their side need to be sufficiently confident of their role to be able fully to acknowledge how much can be gained from partnership with parents. The larger part of the person's day is spent in the home situation. So if the staff are to provide the service which parents are more and more demanding of them, they must have the support of parents. They also need to be provided with reliable information about what goes on in the home and to know that the programmes being developed and applied during the day are welcomed by them. We hope that parents who have worked through this book will seek to create opportunities, in return, to inform staff of their own efforts to help their son/daughter to cope more successfully in the home and local community.

One of the results of a closer contact with professionals will be a better understanding of the difficulties that they face. In our present system, a major source of difficulty is the existence of administrative barriers between the different parts of the service. Mentally handicapped individuals and their families need help, at different stages, from the local Health, Education, and Social Services Departments. Some may also need help from the Housing Department or the Department of Employment. Staff from the various departments need to

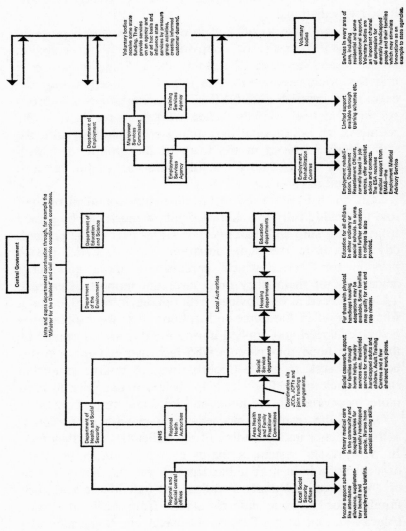

Figure 11. Services for mentally handicapped people in England

Central Government

Intra and extra departmental coordination through, for example the 'Minister for the Disabled' and civil service coordination committees.

Voluntary bodies receive some state funding. They provide services on an agency and or ad hoc basis and influence state services by pressure group activities, creating informed customer demand.

Department of Health and Social Security

Department of the Environment

Department of Education and Science

Department of Employment

Voluntary bodies

Regional and special central offices

NHS

Regional Health Authorities

Manpower Services Commission

Training Services Agency

Employment Services Agency

Local Social Security Offices

Area Health Authorities and Family Practitioner Committees

Coordination via JCCs, JCPTs and joint fundings arrangements.

Local Authorities

Social Service departments

Housing departments

Education departments

Employment Rehabilitation Centres

Income support schemes like attendance allowance, supplementary benefit and unemployment benefits.

Primary medical care in the community and hospital services for mentally handicapped people. Nurses have specialist caring skills.

Social casework, support for families through home helps, laundry services etc. Residential services for mentally handicapped adults and children, Adult Training Centres and a few sheltered work places.

For those with physical handicaps housing adaptations may be available. Some families may qualify for rent and rate rebates.

Education for all children in either ordinary or special schools. In some cases further education in colleges is also provided.

Employment rehabilitation. Disablement Resettlement Officers, normally based in job centres, offer specialist advice and contacts. The ESA receives medical support from EMAS—the Employment Medical Advisory Service

Limited support available through training schemes etc.

Services in every area of care, including residential and some occupational support. Voluntary bodies are an important channel of expression for mentally handicapped people and their families which may stimulate innovations as an example to state agencies.

communicate clearly and to act together in ensuring continuity of provision. But there are often difficulties and delays The National Development Group for the mentally handicapped (NDG) in Pamphlet number 1 states:

> There is good evidence that families find it difficult to find a coordinated service. Planning groups should consider what it is which seems to prevent support services which are often very simple in themselves from reaching overburdened parents. (Para 20, July 1976.)

Understanding and Using the Services
In order to help you to appreciate the overall framework of services, and how they are related to each other, we present in Figure 11 a descriptive chart. (Office of Health Economics).

As you can see, the system is quite complex. The services available for handicapped school-leavers fall under the auspices of various departments. As we see later, the number of options continues to increase, enabling more choices to be made. Government policy has made it clear that the Adult Training Centres (shown as falling under the Social Services Departments) are to become the key resource for habilitation, further training and education of mentally handicapped adults living in the community. Your son or daughter may already be one of the 41,000 trainees currently attending the ATCs.

The 'planning groups' referred to by the NDG (above) are specialised sub-groups which can be set up to advise the Joint Care Planning Teams (see the chart). Most areas now have a JCPT, as suggested in Health Circular 77 (17) and Local Authority Circular 77(10), and most of these have mental handicap sub-groups. The NDG believe that it is

> absolutely crucial that such a sub-group is set up for mental handicap in every area . . . the sub-group must have the widest possible range of membership and should include parents or their representatives as well as those with relevant professional knowledge. (Para 2.)

In the light of this, we suggest that you may wish to make enquiries in your local area about the existence of such a 'Planning Group', and the extent of parental involvement. We believe that you will find many advantages in working as part of an organised group of parents, such as your local branch of the National Society for Mentally Handicapped Children. There are numerous examples of other kinds of groups which parents have formed, catering for different needs, or organising activities of a distinctive kind. A good example of this is 'Kith and Kids', the address of which is listed in the Appendix. They organise ambitious learning programmes which take place with professional support at weekends or during school holidays.

You can probably think immediately of some activities which a parent group in your area could engage in. A general aim could be to support local attempts to coordinate services, for example by devising improved methods of information transfer. Some Local Authorities are experimenting with new systems of record-keeping aimed at ensuring continuity of provision, between the special school and ATC for example. Parents have an important role to play here, not only in contributing their own experience and ideas but also in ensuring that opportunities exist for the views of mentally handicapped individuals involved to be expressed and recorded.

Parents may lend encouragement to the local Authority in drawing up a directory of local facilities and services which mentally handicapped individuals and their families would find useful. If your son/daughter is at the adolescent stage, or is already an adult, your contribution could be aimed at that section of the local directory which is concerned with post-school provision. We have prepared a table of guidance which you could use as a check-list. Examine the extent to which the types of provision listed are to be found in your local area, adding additional items to the list where appropriate.

Table 3: Current Provision

Responsible Agency/Authority	Provision	Population catered for	Description
Department of Education and Science, local education authorities	Specialised curricula in the final year or two of the special schools	ESN(M)/(S) youngsters under 16, or 16 to 19	May include: work orientation, work visits, work related academics, possibly work experience in local firms
	Transitional units	mainly ESN(M) youngsters	Work orientated, simulated work, work related academics, possibly work experience in firms
	Further education colleges	ESN(M)/(S) plus other disabilities	Courses vary in length from three months to two years or more. Basic work habits and skills covered, as well as work experience on campus and often in local firms
Manpower Services Commission			
Training Services Division	Wider Opportunity Courses	For school leavers who have motivational problems and are lacking in self confidence	Three month assessment and training course in TSA Skill Centres
	Occupational Selection Courses	For young people who are said to be in need of social and life skills training, and require occupational guidance	15 week courses of assessment and training

Responsible Agency/Authority	Provision	Population catered for	Description
Employment Service Division	Young Persons' Work Preparation Courses	Educationally disadvantaged school leavers	Three month course of work preparation and remedial education
	Rehabilitation courses in Employment Rehabilitation Centres	Physically and mentally handicapped individuals 16+	7-12 week (maximum 26 week) assessment and rehabilitation course catered to the needs of the individual
Department of health and Social Security, Social Services Provision	Adult Training Centres		Provides assessment, further education, social and work training, no set time period on attendance
National Health Service, subnormality hospital provision	Rehabilitation programmes in subnormality hospitals	All ages and varying degrees of mental handicap	Programme of work preparation includes work orientation, work related academics, work experience within hospital
Voluntary provision: National Society for Mentally Handicapped Children	for example: Lufton Manor	Mentally handicapped adolescents	Rural training
	Pengwern Hall Dilston Hall	Mentally handicapped adolescents and young adults	Work and social training
Village trusts	e.g. Camphill Village Trust	Mentally handicapped, various ages	Living and employment but also preparation for work outside the village

In Conclusion

Society now recognises the rights of mentally handicapped people to take a full place in the community and to be given that extra education and training which they require in order to achieve this. No longer are mentally handicapped people regarded as 'ill'. Theirs is primarily an *educational* problem in the fullest sense of the word. Whereas it was previously recognised that an individual could be trained to perform particular operations or to develop certain skills, the importance is now seen of applying these within a real-life context.

The various objectives of different types of provision must now be justified in terms of their importance to the overall needs of the individual. There can no longer be an over-emphasis on physical needs, in the caring sense, or simply on providing work 'activity'. Full account must now be taken of the individual's emotional and social needs, of their unique individual personality. Educating the whole person also means taking account of his leisure or recreational needs.

As we widen our understanding of what should be provided for an individual, as the range of options available to school leavers are increased, we should also recognise that there is a greater responsibility to exercise judgement in the choices made. It is important that the correct balance should be achieved and care must be taken, for example, that increasing educational opportunities should not be made at the expense of undervaluing the importance of learning to work. In a wider definition of 'education' it can be seen that preparation for work is an important aspect of the overall process, forming as it does a realistic challenge and an opportunity to apply what is being learnt.

Throughout this book we have stressed the importance of involving your son/daughter in the making of decisions which concern him/her. There is some evidence that mentally handicapped young adults experience low self-esteem, and have a higher expectancy of failure. Whilst accepting that horizons will be more limited, we believe that a careful programme of training can succeed in building on the individual's strengths. We have not been concerned simply with his/her ability to cope, we have gone further than this. With your help we have explored the possibility that your son or daughter may experience the satisfaction of being of service to others – rather than remain always on the receiving end. One study likened the life of a mentally handicapped adult to that of a young child in terms of the large number of individuals in positions of authority over him or her, and the small amount of responsibility he or she is free to exercise.

At the end of the book we suggest further reading. We have also made a list of addresses of useful organisations and facilities which you may wish to contact. We include the address of our own Research Centre in this list, and would be glad to hear from you and learn of your experiences in using the ideas in the book. We are also able to send further information concerning our work.

Appendices

1: Programme for a Workshop for Parents of Mentally Handicapped Adolescents and Adults

Held at the Adult Training Centre
Tuesdays: 7.30-9.30 p.m., 11th October, 1977 to
24th January, 1978

This is a workshop for parents of mentally handicapped adolescents and adults. It provides an opportunity for parents to meet together with professionals to explore ways in which more effective cooperation may be achieved. The essence of the workshop approach is that all concerned should contribute their knowledge, experience, and skills.

During the workshop parents will be shown how to assess their own son/daughter, select training goals, and prepare teaching plans to carry out at home. For most sessions, the first half of the evening will involve lectures, films, videotape viewing, and demonstrations. The second half will involve small group work concerned to apply the techniques and ideas to meet individual needs.

Programme

Session	*Date*	*Theme*
1.	11th Oct.	Introduction to the workshop – the parent's role in partnership with the professionals.
2.	18th Oct.	The parent's role in assessment – observing and recording behaviour and progress in the home.
3.	25th Oct.	Adolescent development, including

sexual development, health and hygiene.

4. 1st Nov.   A goal to work towards – how to choose a training objective and break it down into stages.

5. 8th Nov.   Presentation of various methods of training – how to select a method suitable for the objective chosen.

6. 15th Nov. Language development – how to assess common difficulties in speech and language and help to facilitate improvements.

7. 22nd Nov. Employment – what are the prospects and how may they be improved. The role of financial rewards in training.

8. 29th Nov. Social education – especially focussing on those skills which are essential to getting on with other people.

9. 6th Dec.   Further education – a review of some of the areas being taught in the ATC.

10. 13th Dec. Leisure activities – the scope of possible activities, the importance of exercising choice. Educational aspects.

CHRISTMAS BREAK

11. 17th Jan. Open Forum – Questions answered by an invited panel. A multi-disciplinary examination of the needs of parents and the ways in which professionals might respond.

12. 24th Jan. Where do we go from here? An opportunity to explore the possibilities for a closer working partnership with the staff of the ATC and associated professionals.

2: Selective Bibliography

Allen, R. and Cortazzo, A. *Psychosocial and Educational Aspects and Problems of Mental Retardation.* Springfield: Charles C. Thomas. 1970.

Baranyay, E. P. *The Mentally Handicapped Adolescent: the Slough Project of the National Society for Mentally Handicapped Children. An Experimental Step towards Life in the Community.* Pergamon, Oxford. 1971.

Baranyay, E. P. *A Lifetime of Learning.* London: National Society for Mentally Handicapped Children. 1976.

Baroff, G. S. *Mental Retardation, Nature, Cause and Management.* Washington DC: Hemisphere Publishing Corporation. 1974.

Bender, M., Valletutti, P. and Bender, R. *Teaching the Moderately and Severely Handicapped* (in 3 volumes). Baltimore and London: University Park Press. 1976.

Birenbaum, A. and Seiffer, S. *Resettling Retarded Adults in a Managed Community.* 1976.

Brennan, W. K. *Shaping the Education of Slow Learners.* London: Routledge & Kegan Paul. 1974.

Brown, R. I. *Psychology and Education of Slow Learners.* London: Routledge & Kegan Paul. 1976.

Browne, G. *Adjustment to Industry for less able school leavers* – The Bridgend Project. Manchester: National Elfrida Rathbone Society. 1977.

Clark, D. F. *Mental Deficiency: The Changing Outlook.* London: Methuen & Co. Ltd. 1974.

Clarke, A. D. B. and Clarke, A. M. *Recent Advances in the Study of Subnormality.* London: National Association of Mental Health. 1974.

Department of Employment. *Handicapped School Leavers Work Preparation Course,* Paper No. 2. London: Department of Employment. 1974.

Elliott, J. and Whelan E. *Employment of Mentally Handi-*

H

capped People. Mental Handicap Paper No. 8. London: King's Fund Centre.

Fernald, W. E. After-care study of patients discharged from Waverly for a period of 25 years. 1919.

Gardner, W. I. *Behaviour Modification in Mental Retardation: the Education and Rehabilitation of the Mentally Retarded Adolescent and Adult.* London: Univ. London Press. 1971.

Gold, M. W. *Research on the vocational habilitation of the retarded: the present, the future.* In: International Review of Research into Mental Retardation, vol. 6. 1973.

Gold, M. W. *Try Another Way.* Indianapolis: Film Productions of Indianapolis. 1975.

Gunzburg, H. C. *Social Rehabilitation of the Subnormal.* London: Bailliere, Tindall & Cox. 1960.

Jordan, T. E. *The Mentally Retarded.* Columbus, Ohio: Charles C. Merrill Publishing Co. 1972.

Kedney, R. and Whelan E. *The Education of Mentally Handicapped Young Adults.* Bolton: Bolton College of Education (Technical). 1977.

King's Fund Centre. *Adult Education for Mentally Handicapped People.* KFC, London (Mental Handicap Paper 6). 1975.

Kirk, S. *Educating Exceptional Children.* Boston: Houghton & Mifflin. 1972.

Kirman, B. H. *Mental Retardation: some recent developments in the study of causes and social effects of this problem.* Pergamon Press (written for parents). 1970.

Manpower Services Commission Employment Service Agency. *Rehabilitation, Retraining and Resettlement.* Birmingham: HMSO. 1976.

Manpower Services Commission. *Young People and Work.* London: Manpower Services Commission. 1977.

Marshall, A. *The Abilities and Attainments of Children Leaving Junior Training Centres.* London: National Association for Mental Health. 1967.

Mattinson, J. *Marriage and Mental Handicap.* London: Duckworth. 1970.

Mittler, P. J. *Assessment for Learning in the Mentally Handicapped.* Edinburgh & London: Churchill Livingstone. 1973.

Mittler, P. J. and Gittens, D. *The Educational Needs of Mentally Handicapped Adults.* Manchester: National Society for Mentally Handicapped Children. 1974.

Mittler, P. J. (ed). *The Psychological Assessment of Mental and Physical Handicaps.* London: Tavistock Publications in Association with Methuen & Co. Ltd. 1974.

Mittler, P. J. (ed). *Research to Practice in Mental Retardation* – Vol. 2, Education and Training. Baltimore: University Park Press. 1977.

National Development Group for the Mentally Handicapped. *Helping Mentally Handicapped School Leavers.* London: HMSO. 1977.

National Development Group for the Mentally Handicapped. *Day Services for Mentally Handicapped Adults.* London; HMSO. 1977.

Office of Health Economics. *Mental Handicap: ways forward.* London: OHE, 162, Regent Street. 1978.

Posner, B. Changing Attitudes Toward Retarded People. Paper delivered to Canadian Conference on Mental Retardation. 1972.

Reiter, S. *Vocational Counselling of Mentally Handicapped Adults.* Unpublished Ph.D. thesis. University of Manchester. 1975.

Schlesinger, H. and Whelan E. (in collaboration with Rosan, M. and Davies, S.). *Industry and Effort – A Study of Work Centres in England, Wales and Northern Ireland, for the Severely Disabled.* Report to the Spastics Society. London (to be published): 1978.

Speake, B. R. and Whelan, E. *Young Persons Work Preparation Courses: A Systematic Evaluation.* London: Manpower Services Commission. 1977.

Sternlich, M. and Deutsch, M. *Personality, Development and*

Social Behaviour in the Mentally Retarded. Lexington, Massachusetts: Lexington Books. 1972.

Stevens, H. A. and Heber R. *Mental Retardation.* Chicago: University of Chicago Press. 1964.

Tansley, A. E. and Gulliford, R. *The Education of Slow Learning Children.* London: Routledge & Kegan Paul. 1960.

Tuckey, L., Parfitt J. and Tuckey B. *Handicapped School-Leavers: Their Further Education, Training and Employment.* London: National Foundation for Educational Research. 1973.

Warnock, H. M. *Special Educational Needs. Report of the Committee of Enquiry into the Education of Handicapped Children and Young People.* London: HMSO. 1978.

Whelan, E. and Speake, B. R. *Adult Training Centres in England and Wales – Report of the First National Survey.* Manchester: National Association of Teachers of the Mentally Handicapped. 1977.

Wolfensberger, W. *The Principle of Normalization in Human Services.* Toronto: National Institute on Mental Retardation. 1972.

Zisfein. L. and Rosen M. *Personal Adjustment Training: A Group Counselling Program for Institutionalized Mentally Retarded Persons.* Mental Retardation. 1973.

3. Information Sources

Careers Research and Advisory Centre,
Bateman Street,
Cambridge CB2 1LZ

Centre on Environment for the Handicapped,
120-126 Albert Street,
London NW1 7NE

Centre for Information and Advice on Educational
Disadvantage,
14 Anson Road,
Manchester M14 5BY

Citizens Advice Bureau,
National Head Office,
26 Bedford Square,
London WC1

The King's Fund Centre,
Albert Street,
London NW1 7NE

Learning Development Aids,
(Materials for Children with learning difficulties)
Park Works,
Norwich Road,
Wisbech, Cambs. PE13 2AH

Toy Libraries Association,
Sunley House,
Gunthorpe Street,
London E1 7RW

Health Education Council,
78 New Oxford Street,
London WC1A 1AA

National Foundation for Educational Research,
Publishing Company,
Darville House,
2 Oxford Road,
Windsor, Berks. SL4 1DF
(for information on assessment scales for young children).

4. Associations for Mental Handicap

American Association on Mental Deficiency,
5201 Connecticut Avenue N.W.,
Washington D.C. 20015

Association for Professions for the Mentally Handicapped,
Albert Street,
London

Association for the Retarded in Wales,
c/o Dr Rogie Angus,
30 College Road,
Bangor, Gwynedd LL57 1AN

British Association for the Retarded,
17 Pembridge Square,
London W2 4EP

Campaign for the Mentally Handicapped,
96 Portland Place,
London W1N 4EX

The Home Farm Trust Ltd.,
(Registered Charity for the Mentally Handicapped)
Registered Office,
57 Queen Square,
Bristol

Kith and Kids,
Maurice Collins,
58 The Avenue,
London N10

National Association of Mental Health (MIND),
22 Harley Street,
London

The National Association of Teachers of the Mentally
Handicapped,
Mrs E. Hughes,
1 Beechfield Avenue,
Urmston,
Manchester

National Elfrida Rathbone Society
(National Office)
83 Mosley Street,
Manchester M2 3L6

(Northern Office)
229 Woodhouse Lane,
Leeds 2

(Midlands Office)
14 Stoneleigh Avenue,
Earlsden,
Coventry CV5 6BZ

National Federation of Gateway Clubs,
21 Star Street,
London W2

National Society for Mentally Handicapped Children,
Pembridge Hall,
17 Pembridge Square,
London W2 4EP

NSMHC – Regional Offices

1. *Eastern Counties Region,*
   63a Churchgate Street,
   Bury St Edmunds,
   Suffolk 1P33 1RL

2. *East Midlands Region,*
   32 Park Row,
   Nottingham NG1 6GR

3. *Home Counties North Region,*
   5 College Street,
   St Albans,
   Herts.

4. *Metropolitan Region*
   Coventry House,
   5/6 Coventry Street,
   London W1

5. *Northern Region*
   20 North Terrace,
   Claremont Road,
   Newcastle upon Tyne NE2 4AD

6. *North West Region*
   1 Brazennose Street,
   Manchester M2 5FJ

7. *South East Region*
   34 Surrey Street,
   Croydon CR9 1JU

8. *South Wales and Monmouthshire Region*
   31 The Parade,
   Cardiff CF2 3AD

9. *South West Region*
   17 High Street,
   Taunton,
   Somerset

10. *West Midlands Region*
    21 Guildhall Buildings,
    Navigation Street,
    Birmingham B2 4BT

11. *Yorkshire Region*
    11 Station Square,
    Harrogate,
    Yorks.

12. *Northern Ireland Region*
    4 Annadale Avenue,
    Belfast BT7 3JH

Scottish Society for the Mentally Handicapped,
69 West Regent Street,
Glasgow G2

5. Other Useful Associations

Association for Spina Bifida and Hydrocephalus,
Devonshire Street House,
Devonshire Street,
London W1N ZEB

British Council for Rehabilitation of the Disabled,
Tavistock House South,
Tavistock Square,
London WC1H 9LB

British Epilepsy Association,
3-6 Alfred Place,
London WC1E 7EE

British Sports Association for the Disabled,
Stoke Mandeville Stadium,
Harvey Road,
Aylesbury,
Bucks. HP21 8PP

Central Council for the Disabled,
34 Eccleston Square,
London SW1V 1PE

Disabled Living Foundation,
346 Kensington High Street,
London W14 8NS

National Bureau for Handicapped Students,
City of London Polytechnic,
Calcutta House Precinct,
Old Castle Street,
London E1 7NT

National Children's Bureau,
8 Wakely Street,
London EC1V 7QE

The Spastics Society,
12 Park Crescent,
London W1N 4EA

Voluntary Council for Handicapped Children,
National Children's Bureau,
8 Wakely Street,
London EC1V 7QE

6. Government Bodies

DES (Department of Education and Science) Publications
and DHSS (Department of Health and Social Security)
Publications,
Government Buildings,
Honeypot Lane,
Stanmore,
Middlesex

Department of Health and Social Security,
Information Division,
Alexander Fleming House,
London SE1

Employment Service Division,
7 St Martin's Place,
London

Manpower Services Commission,
Selkirk House,
166 High Holborn,
London WC1V 6PF

National Development Group for the Mentally Handicapped,
Department of Health and Social Security,
Alexander Fleming House,
Elephant and Castle,
London

7. Research Bodies

British Society for the Study of Mental Subnormality,
Monyhull Hospital,
Birmingham

Elwyn Institute,
Elwyn,
Pennsylvania,
USA

Health Care Evaluation Research Team,
Highcroft,
Romsey Road,
Winchester,
Hampshire

Institute for Research into Mental and Multiple Handicap,
16 Fitzroy Square,
London W1P 5HQ

Institute of Mental Subnormality,
Wolverhampton Road,
Kidderminster,
Worcester DY10 3PP

Mental Handicap in Wales,
Applied Research Unit,
Ely Hospital,
Cowbridge Road West,
Cardiff CF 5XE

Thomas Coram Research Unit,
41 Brunswick Square,
London WC1N 1AZ

Vocational Rehabilitation and Research Institute,
3304 3354 N.W,
Calgary 44,
Alberta,
Canada